More Praise for *Love 'Em or Lose 'Em*

"You just have to love *Love 'Em or Lose 'Em*. This charming, clever, practical, and user-friendly book is a great deskside coach for anyone who manages people."
—**Rosabeth Moss Kanter, Chair and Director, Advanced Leadership Initiative, Harvard University**

"Talent matters. Few dispute this truth. But keeping great talent continues to be a challenge for many companies. This marvelous book offers numerous specific tools and hundreds of examples of how to care for people. *Love 'Em or Lose 'Em* is the best treatise on retaining talent available."
—**Dave Ulrich, Professor, Ross School of Business, University of Michigan, and coauthor of *HR from the Outside In: Six Competencies for the Future of Human Resources***

"Fantastic, fun, and practical coaching advice! This stuff works! Great for executives to use with their teams—and buy for their managers! Buy it! Use it! Share it! Keep good people."
—**Marshall Goldsmith, author of *Mojo: How to Get It, How to Keep It, How to Get It Back If You Lose It***

"The manager-employee relationship is the difference between retention and turnover. Good leaders know how to hold on to their team members by striking a balance between leadership and management. The trick is to publicly praise employees for their victories and privately coach them on their opportunities. *Love 'Em or Lose 'Em* helps create the foundation for doing just that."
—**Ken May, former President and CEO, FedEx Kinko's**

"At First Data, the *Love 'Em or Lose 'Em* concepts have become an integral part of our ongoing global retention and engagement strategy and one of our most widely attended manager training programs. The book is full of practical employee engagement strategies, coaching, and advice that can be easily applied by any manager and applicable to employees at all levels. With the additional global perspectives in this newest edition, the relevance of the *Love 'Em or Lose 'Em* messages is now truly boundaryless."
—**Michelle Prince, Vice President, Human Resources, First Data**

"A great read! Having had the opportunity to spend two days in a 'Love 'Em or Lose 'Em' seminar, I am a believer! It makes no difference what business you are in (corporate/government/military), people are the single most important part of an organization, and they are at the core of the success or failure of an organization!"
—**William (Bill) Pickavance, former Vice President for Launch and Recovery Systems and Florida Site Executive, United Space Alliance**

"I'm a big fan of the 'stay interview' and its power; nothing speaks louder than a manager who genuinely cares. That's just one great idea from this latest edition of *Love 'Em or Lose 'Em*, which should be on every manager's bookshelf or tablet or smart phone!"
—**Rebecca Ray, Senior Vice President of Human Capital, The Conference Board**

"I have long believed love is at the deepest center of leading oneself and others, and to find a book that provides specific and practical ways for managers to pay attention to their talent is truly a gift. How one leads is a choice, and in this gem of a read are powerful reminders of how managers can show up and be present to their people, particularly if they want to bring out the best in others, keeping them engaged and inspired to stay and contribute to their fullest potential. This book deserves to be read at least once a year or kept nearby as a guide."
—**Teresa Roche, Vice President and Chief Learning Officer, Agilent Technologies**

"I found the authors' approach to be very practical with many ideas I can put to use immediately. This book helped me adjust my understanding of American management principles."
—**Hiroyuki Hirano, General Manager, Suzuyo & Co., Ltd**

"I've been so impressed with the millennials entering our workforce around the world. This book is full of great tips for getting their best discretionary effort—love them and you will be a beloved manager."
—**Tina Sung, Vice President, Government Transformation and Agency Partnerships, Partnership for Public Service**

"Ever since the first edition, *Love 'Em or Lose 'Em* has been a great source of inspiration to me. I warmly recommend this pragmatic book to anyone who manages others—and especially to those who still believe that talent retention is all about money, which it is really not! This book offers a powerful and engaging way to achieve active and sustainable talent retention. And it's exciting to see that it works all across the globe!"
—**Michael Zollinger, Head HR Generalists, Swiss Re**

"Marriott's global engagement strategy includes asking associates worldwide about their work environment and then providing resources to guide them through the key drivers of engagement and retention in the workplace. As a global resource in Marriott's engagement strategy, Kaye and Jordan-Evans once again provide a powerful, globally inclusive book that is both impactful and relevant . . . practical, associate-centric ideas that work!"
—**Steve Bauman, Vice President, Global Learning Deployment, Marriott International**

"If you need a practical and effective way to retain and engage your talent, look no further than *Love 'Em or Lose 'Em*: the A to Z for managers and leaders who care about their employees enough to take action that delivers results. Having witnessed, firsthand, the power of the 'stay interview' and the impact of simply asking employees what will keep them in the organization, I know the rewards contained within *Love 'Em or Lose 'Em* are easily attained. Finding talent can be hard in today's competitive world. Keeping that talent can be deceptively easy."
—**Andrew Buckingham, Head of Global Learning and Development, Genzyme UK**

"Our global strategy is based on recruiting and developing the best talent. Retaining and engaging that talent on a global basis is crucial to every manager's business goals. *Love 'Em or Lose 'Em* has become their playbook. Our managers believe in the concept and their behaviors are consistent—it has become part of our lexicon. And most importantly, employees are responding!"
—**J. Craig Mundy, Corporate Vice President, Enterprise Learning & Talent Management, Ingersoll Rand**

"*Love 'Em or Lose 'Em* has significantly contributed to our business in Latin America by setting ground rules and providing practical tools and techniques to our leaders who constantly transform our organization. The wonderful principles in this book have raised our sensitivity on how to interpret our associates' needs, and once put in practice, they have enabled powerful results. It is a very dynamic and updated consultation book I have valued throughout my career at Pepsico."
—**Carolina Lazarte, Human Resources Director, Latin America North, D&I LAB, Pepsico Latin America Beverages**

LOVE 'EM

or LOSE 'EM

Other Berrett-Koehler books by:

Beverly Kaye and Sharon Jordan-Evans

Love It, Don't Leave It: 26 Ways to Get What You Want at Work

Beverly Kaye and Julie Winkle Guilioni

Help Them Grow or Watch Them Go

LOVE 'EM or LOSE 'EM

GETTING GOOD PEOPLE TO STAY

Fifth Edition

BEVERLY KAYE AND SHARON JORDAN–EVANS

Berrett–Koehler Publishers, Inc.
a BK Business book

Berrett-Koehler Publishers, Inc.
1333 Broadway, Suite 1000
Oakland, CA 94612-1921
Tel: (510) 817-2277   Fax: (510) 817-2278   www.bkconnection.com

Ordering information for print editions
Quantity sales. Special discounts are available on quantity purchases by corporations, associations, and others. For details, contact the "Special Sales Department" at the Berrett-Koehler address above.

Individual sales. Berrett-Koehler publications are available through most bookstores. They can also be ordered directly from Berrett-Koehler: Tel: (800) 929-2929; Fax: (802) 864-7626; www.bkconnection.com

Orders for college textbook/course adoption use. Please contact Berrett-Koehler: Tel: (800) 929-2929; Fax: (802) 864-7626.

Distributed to the U.S. trade and internationally by Penguin Random House Publisher Services.

Berrett-Koehler and the BK logo are registered trademarks of Berrett-Koehler Publishers, Inc.

Printed in the United States of America

Berrett-Koehler books are printed on long-lasting acid-free paper. When it is available, we choose paper that has been manufactured by environmentally responsible processes. These may include using trees grown in sustainable forests, incorporating recycled paper, minimizing chlorine in bleaching, or recycling the energy produced at the paper mill.

Library of Congress Cataloging-in-Publication Data

Kaye, Beverly L.
    Love 'em or lose 'em : getting good people to stay / Beverly Kaye and
Sharon Jordan-Evans. — Fifth edition.
        pages   cm
    Includes bibliographical references and index.
    ISBN 978-1-60994-884-9 (pbk.)
    1. Employee retention. 2. Labor turnover. I. Jordan-Evans, Sharon, 1946–
II. Title.
HF5549.5.R58K39 2014
658.3'14—dc23
                                                            2013038755

Fifth Edition
25 24 23 22 21 20 19   17 16 15 14 13 12 11

Production management and editorial services: Michael Bass Associates
Cover design and interior art: Tracy Rocca
Interior design: Seventeenth Street Studios

To my beloved parents. Abe and Mollie Kaye truly lived a seven-decade love story. They inspired me personally and professionally throughout my life and are truly missed!

—Bev

To my kids and their kids. You continue to teach me what "lovin' 'em" is all about. I do love you!

—Sharon

CONTENTS

LOVE 'EM OR LOSE 'EM
A PROVEN APPROACH TO LEADING

It's a power button...

For over a decade we've watched leaders at all levels and in all parts of the globe use a love 'em approach to building loyal, committed, productive teams. All that in an era when some said (incorrectly) that loyalty is dead. Their employees cannot be enticed away by a 10 percent raise or a gym or a massage on Fridays. They *love* their jobs, their teams, their bosses, and yes, their companies. And because of that, their companies win.

...not a toggle switch

In contrast, we've seen leaders lose talent regularly and unnecessarily. In some cases these not-so-successful leaders matched their engagement and retention efforts to economic highs and lows. In the good times, when jobs were plentiful and talented people had choice, managers offered perks, praise, and promotions. In bad times, these leaders developed a cavalier attitude about their employees. Many felt—and some actually said—"Quit whining—be glad you have a job." In every case, they failed to use the love 'em approach.

So what is the love 'em approach in a nutshell? It's a mindset, a philosophy of dealing with people and a way of effectively managing them. Some people told us the word *love* would not be accepted in the business world.

We tried, and we failed to find an alternative—another word that stood for so much. Love 'em leaders genuinely care about their people. They appreciate, nurture, grow, recognize, challenge, understand, and respect them. And they believe this *is* the job of being a leader.

In contrast, *non–love 'em* leaders are more apt to ignore their employees, tell them what to do and when to do it, expect obedience, fail to respect them, thank them, challenge them, care about them. Ultimately, they believe the love 'em approach is *not* part of their job.

What's the payoff with the love 'em approach?

You might wonder why you'd bother to care more, listen more, develop more. What's in it for you? For the organization? Whether you manage one or hundreds of people, our research and others' definitively show that you can influence those things that keep people engaged, on your team, and producing at their peak. You have more power and influence in the employee engagement and retention equation than anyone else! And engaged, highly productive employees help you, your team, and your organization excel.

Four important words that drive the message

Readers of our book (this is our fifth edition) have loved the title *Love 'Em or Lose 'Em: Getting Good People to Stay*. But it's not just a catchy title. The words drive the heart of our message. Here's how we're using these words:

Love

It's easy. Treat employees fairly and respectfully. Listen to them. Help them get what they want and need. Thank them. Challenge and develop them. Care about them, and you will engage and retain them.

Lose

Loss is just as serious when talent retires on the job as when they leave to join a competitor.

Good

Consider your solid citizens, not just your high-potentials. Stars are people at any level who bring value to the organization.

Stay

Encourage talented employees to stay with the enterprise (if not your own department). Talent will be the key differentiating factor in the competitive battle ahead.

Research Base

Global research supports this approach. We use exit interview information, focus groups, and the Internet. We (and dozens of helpers) continually scan newspapers, journals, and books. We deliver the love 'em message to managers worldwide, and we learn *directly from them and from their employees*—what works and what doesn't.

We ask the question "What kept you?" everywhere.

Our analysis of that data helped us form the original 26 strategies and chapters A–Z. We've built on that original research, meeting with more than half a million managers from large and small companies around the world. We've listened, consulted, provided training, and learned from them. We continually update our "What Kept You" database (more than 18,000 respondents). All of this helps us refine and expand our engagement and retention strategies.

What's in this book for you?

Love 'Em is universal.

The suggestions throughout the book should work as well in India as they do in Idaho, with appropriate customization for cultural, language, or individual differences.

Love 'Em is timeless.

The love 'em approach works as well in 2020 (we plan to be around!) as in 1999 (first edition).

Love 'Em is timely.

For the fifth edition, we've updated the stories, statistics, and workplace views so that they are relevant for you as a manager now.

Updated content for you:

- Practical to-do lists

- Multiple business examples about what worked to engage and retain talent around the globe

- Real-life "alas" stories about losing solid performers

New for you:

- More stats, stories, and cultural references from global contributors

- A *ponderable* at the beginning of every chapter, to introduce key themes and to spark your thinking

- A "Calling All Managers of Managers" section in the back matter, to highlight what leaders can do to strengthen the engagement/retention skills of the managers who report to them

We've *kept* the navigation tools in the book that you find helpful:

- Helpful "go to" icons linking to more ideas about what interests you most

- A retention/engagement index (REI) to guide your learning (moved to the beginning of the book so you won't miss it!)

Make this yours

We wrote *Love 'Em or Lose 'Em* to make your life easier, to help you in a real-time, day-to-day way. We wrote it because you make such an impact on the lives of your workforce. That's an awesome responsibility that deserves all the help and support it can get.

★ Create and implement your own, unique version of the love 'em approach.

★ Use this as your guide—as you would use a GPS.

★ Return to it again and again.

★ Dog-ear the page corners.

★ Use a highlighter on what matters most to you.

★ Put a bookmark in key chapters, and leave the book on your own manager's desk!

★ Personally commit to implementing the key message of just one chapter. Start by reading Ask and Buck—then go anywhere you want.

Bottom line: make the love 'em approach your daily practice

The *Love 'Em or Lose 'Em* approach to engaging and retaining talent is not something you turn on and off, syncing to the latest economic blip and the corresponding concern about keeping talent.

It works best when it's authentic and perennial, when you clearly believe in it and demonstrate it daily in your actions with the people you want on your team.

Talent is everything. As a manager, you know that. You need your talented people to stay with you. These people are critical to your success. And your competitors want them!

So how will you keep them engaged? Excited about coming to work and performing at their peak? How will you get them to stay (both psychologically and physically) while others try to entice them away? *Love 'Em or Lose 'Em* will show you how.

HOW TO READ THIS BOOK

How do *you* like to read a book? Start at the beginning and read to the end? Start at the end, and then circle back to the beginning? Skim, scan, and then dive in when a topic really grabs your interest? Any of these approaches will work fine with *Love 'Em or Lose 'Em*.

In any case, we'd recommend you read Ask and Buck early, as these two chapters support all the others. They introduce you to the love 'em approach, teach you how to hold stay interviews, and get you thinking about the crucial role you play in the engagement/retention challenge.

We also suggest you take just a few moments to check out your beliefs about managing, engaging, and retaining others by completing a manager self-test called The Retention/Engagement Index (REI). The results will direct you to chapters you might want to read soon.

What's Your REI?

Research shows that your perspectives and beliefs about managing others and the resulting actions you take can predict the likelihood that talented people will not only continue to work for you but will bring their discretionary effort to work each and every day. They'll help you and your organization do what you're trying to do!

This survey allows you to evaluate your beliefs and mindsets about engaging and retaining the people you can least afford to lose.

Use this scale to rate yourself (1–4) on the extent to which you believe or act in the ways listed here.

1 = Always/Definitely Yes
2 = Often/Frequently
3 = Sometimes/Occasionally
4 = Never/Definitely No

	To what extent do you . . .	Score (1–4)
A.	assume that employees should and will tell you what they want from their work?	
B.	believe that retention is a job for HR or compensation professionals?	
C.	regard employees' careers as their business, not yours?	
D.	take for granted that employees know you respect them, and therefore you don't need to show it?	
E.	think employees should tell you if they are not feeling challenged in their work?	
F.	expect employees to leave their personal lives at the door and feel only their business lives are your concern?	
G.	avoid discussing career options with employees, especially when promotions are not readily available?	
H.	hire primarily based on functional or technical skills?	
I.	give information to employees on a need-to-know basis only?	
J.	think you are here to get the job done, that employees don't have to like you?	
K.	believe you are not at work to have fun?	
L.	fear that if you introduce employees to others in your network, they might be enticed away?	
M.	feel that you don't have time to mentor?	
N.	have only a vague idea of what it costs to lose talented people?	
O.	tend to hoard good people instead of helping them seek other opportunities?	
P.	agree that we don't have the luxury of loving what we do?	
Q.	fail to question policies for the sake of your employees?	
R.	deem good work to be its own reward?	
S.	think that if you don't control the who, how, where, and when, the work won't be done right?	
T.	avoid giving negative or corrective feedback to your employees?	

To what extent do you . . .		Score (1–4)
U.	consider yourself too busy to be a good listener?	
V.	view employees' values as their own business and therefore seldom discuss them?	
W.	believe that employee wellness initiatives are frills?	
X.	think that generational differences are irrelevant in the workplace?	
Y.	believe employees should usually wait for you to tell them what to do?	
Z.	maintain that employee engagement and retention are not critical leadership skills and you don't need to spend time improving them?	

So, how did you do? Here is how to make sense of the test, gauge your overall strength as a love 'em manager, and decide which chapters to read first.

1. **Highlight beliefs or behaviors for which you scored a 1 or 2.**

2. **Turn to the corresponding A–Z chapter.**

3. **Pick up some hints and tips about how to increase your effectiveness in those areas.**

Now, note how you're doing overall by adding up your total score and using these interpretation guidelines:

High 80–104: *Good job. You have the love 'em mindset and are probably taking many of the actions needed to engage and retain your talent.*

Medium 53–79: *Beware. You're at risk for losing your best people. Some may have already left you. Take stock and take action before you lose more talent.*

Low 26–52: *Look out! You're at high risk for losing talent—you might even have a "swinging door." Your beliefs and corresponding actions (or inactions) may be standing in the way of having engaged people who want to stick around and work for you over time. You need to take immediate, focused action.*

This book exists to help you increase your score—the one you just gave yourself in this self-test—and the one your employees give you every day.

When your REI goes up, so do your talented employees' job satisfaction levels, motivation, and loyalty.

Time to dive in!

ONE

WHAT KEEPS YOU?

Ponder this: Do you know what they really want?

When do you think most leaders ask questions like "What can I do to keep you?"

You're right: it's in the exit interview. At that point it's typically too late. The talented employee already has one foot out the door!

Have you ever wondered why we ask great questions in exit interviews but neglect to ask early enough to make a difference? Love 'em leaders do ask. They ask early and often, they listen carefully to the answers, and they link arms with their talent to help them get more of what they want, right where they are.

Conduct Stay Interviews

A crucial strategy for engaging and retaining talent is having conversations with every person you hope will stay on your team. We coined the term *stay interview* to describe those chats. If you hold stay interviews, you'll have less regrettable turnover and fewer exit interviews!

When we suggest asking employees why they stay or what would keep them, we hear, "You've got to be kidding," "Isn't that illegal?" or "What if they give me an answer I don't want to hear?" Managers dance around this core subject usually for one of three reasons:

- Some managers fear putting people on the spot or putting ideas into their heads (as if they never thought about leaving on their own).

- Some managers are afraid they will be unable to do anything anyway, so why ask? They fear that the question will raise more dust than they can settle and may cause employees to expect answers and solutions that are out of the managers' hands.

- Some managers say they don't have the time to have these critical one-on-one discussions with their talented people. There is an urgency to produce, leaving little time to listen, let alone ask. (If you don't have time for these discussions with the people who contribute to your success, where will you find the time to interview, select, orient, and train their replacements?)

Guessing Is Risky

What if you don't ask? What if you just keep trying to guess what Tara or Mike or Akina really wants? You will guess right sometimes. The year-end bonus might please them all. Money can inspire loyalty and commitment for the near term. But if the key to retaining Tara is to give her a chance to learn something new, whereas Mike wants to telecommute, how could you ever guess that? Ask—so you don't have to guess.

Alas *A senior manager told us of an employee who was leaving his company. On her last day, the senior manager, who was upset at the loss, expressed his disappointment that she was leaving. He wished her well but said, "I wish there were something we could have done to keep you," assuming that her direct supervisor had asked what would make her stay. But the supervisor hadn't asked, and something could have been done. The employee said she would have stayed if she could have been more involved in some of the new task forces, as she felt the participation was vital to her goal of growing her career. It was a request that would have been easy to fill—if only he had known!*

Asking has positive side effects. The person you ask will feel cared about, valued, and important. Many times asking leads to stronger loyalty and commitment to you and the organization. In other words, just asking the question is an effective engagement and retention strategy.

How to Ask

How and when do you bring up this topic? How can you increase the odds of getting honest input from your employees? There is no single way or time to ask. It could happen during a developmental or career discussion with your employees. (You do hold those, don't you?) Or you might schedule a meeting with your valued employees for the express purpose of finding out what will keep them. One manager sent the following invitation to give his key people some time to think and to prepare for the conversation:

You are invited to attend . . .

. . . the next step in your continued development.
You make a difference and I value your contributions.
Let's discuss some things that are important to you and me:

What will keep you here?

What might entice you away?

What is most energizing about your work?

Are we fully using your talents?

What is inhibiting your success?

What can I do differently to best assist you?

Please schedule a meeting with me within the next two weeks
to discuss this and anything else you'd like to talk about.

Regardless of when you start this dialogue, remember to set the context by telling your employees how critical they are to you and your team and how important it is to you that they stay. Then find out what will keep them. Listen carefully to their responses.

He Dared to Ask

Charlie set up a meeting with his plant manager, Ken, for Monday morning. After some brief conversation about the weekend activities, Charlie said, "Ken, you are critical to me and to this organization. I'm not sure I've told you that directly or often enough. But you are. I can't imagine losing you. So, I'd like to know what will keep you here. And what might entice you away?"

Ken was a bit taken aback—but felt flattered. He thought for a moment and then said, "You know, I aspire to move up in the organization at some point, and I'd love to have some exposure to the senior team. I'd like to see how they operate, and frankly I'd like them to get to know me, too." Charlie responded, "I could take you with me to some senior staff meetings. Would that be a start?" Ken said, "That would be great."

Charlie delivered on Ken's request one week later.

What If—

What If You Can't Give What They Want?

Most managers don't ask because they fear one of two responses: a request for a raise or a promotion. They might not be able to deliver on those kinds of requests. Then what?

Next time a talented employee asks for something you think you might not be able to give, respond by using these four steps:

1. Restate how much you value them.

2. Tell the truth about the obstacles you face in granting their requests.

3. Show you care enough to look into their requests and to stand up for them.

4. Ask, "What else?"

Here's how the discussion between Charlie and Ken could have gone if Ken had asked for a raise.

Following Charlie's question about what will keep him, Ken replied immediately, "A 20 percent raise will do it!" Now, some managers will say things like "Are you kidding? You're already at the top of your pay range." That response shuts down the dialogue and makes a key employee feel less than key. Charlie was ready for this possibility, though. Here is how he could have responded to Ken's request for a raise, using the four-step process.

1. *"You are worth that and more to me.*

2. *I'd love to say yes, but I will need to investigate the possibility. I'm honestly not sure what I can do immediately, given some recent budget cuts.*

3. *But I hear your request. I'll run this up the flag pole and get back to you by next Friday with some answers and a possible time line for a raise.*

4. *Meanwhile, Ken, what else matters to you? What else are you hoping for?"*

Ken might have responded with his interest in getting to know the senior team— and Charlie was ready to act on that one immediately.

GO TO
Understand
page 206

Research shows clearly that people want more from work than just a paycheck. When you ask the question "What else?" we guarantee there will be at least one thing your talented employee wants that you can give. Remember to listen actively as your employees talk about what will keep them on your team or in your organization.

What If You Ask What They Want and They Say, "I Don't Know?"

Remember that this is not an interrogation—it's a conversation, and hopefully one in an ongoing series of conversations. It's okay not to know. Some people will be surprised by your questioning and need some time to think about it. Let them think, schedule another meeting, and set the stage for an ongoing dialogue about your employees' wants, needs, and career goals. Engaging and keeping your talent is a process, not an event.

What If They Don't Trust You Enough to Answer Honestly?

Discussions like these build trust. Ironically, discussions like these *require* trust. If your employees are afraid to answer your questions for any reason, you may need to build a trusting relationship with them before you can expect honest, heartfelt responses. Try to discover why trust is missing in the relationship, and purposely act in trust-building ways. Seek help from colleagues, human resource professionals, or coaches.

What If They Question Your Motivation or Smile and Say, "What Book Have You Just Read?"

Be honest. If you're not in the habit of having dialogues like these, it could feel strange—for you and perhaps for them. Tell them you *did* read a book or attend a course about engaging talent, and you did it because they matter to you. Tell them you honestly want to hear their answers and you want to partner with them to help them get what they want and need. You might even choose to admit that the love 'em approach sometimes feels awkward, even uncomfortable (like a new pair of shoes). That "name it to claim it," forthright action can be just what's needed to build trust with the talent you hope will stay and play on your team.

To Do

★ Ask each employee what will keep him or her at your company or your department.

★ Make a note in your computer or smartphone for every employee's answer.

★ Every month, review the notes and ask yourself what you've done for that employee that relates to his or her needs.

Why Most Say They Stay

We've asked over 18,000 people why they stayed in an organization for "a while" (yes, it's a relative term). Our findings confirm what many others (e.g., Blessing White, Gallup, Towers Watson, Sirota) have learned about the most common reasons employees remain at a company (and what will help retain them). The items recur throughout every industry and at every level. The differences between functions, levels, genders, geographic regions, and ages are minor. Here are the top 13 responses listed in order of frequency of response as of November 2013.

1. Exciting, challenging, or meaningful work

2. Supportive management/good boss

3. Being recognized, valued, and respected

4. Career growth, learning, and development

5. Flexible work environment

6. Fair pay

7. Job location

8. Job security and stability

9. Pride in the organization, its mission or product

10. Working with great coworkers or clients

11. Fun, enjoyable work environment

12. Good benefits

13. Loyalty and commitment to coworkers or boss

How do your employees' answers compare with the list? Find out what truly matters to them by asking. Then create customized, innovative approaches to retaining your talent.

By the way, if you'd like to see the complete "What Kept You" survey data, including updated findings and multiple demographic breakdowns, go to our website, www.keepem.com and click on the "What Kept You" link.

A Word about Pay

Some of you immediately noticed the fact that fair pay lands in seventh place on this list. Here is what we know about pay. If employees see compensation as noncompetitive, unfair, or simply insufficient to sustain life, their dissatisfaction levels will go up. Your talented people will become vulnerable to talent theft or will begin looking around for something better, especially in a favorable job market. But here's the rub. While it can be a huge dissatisfier if inadequate, even fair pay won't keep people who are unhappy in other key areas.

So if your talented people do not feel challenged, or grown, or cared about, a big paycheck will not keep them for long. Researchers over time have found this to be true. Frederic Herzberg found in the 1950s that pay is a "hygiene factor"—make sure it's there or it will be noticed![1] So, do what you can as a manager to influence your organization's compensation programs. Be sure they are competitive and fair—then focus on *what else* you can do to keep your talent.

A Word About Culture

How do cultural differences play out in this crucial, foundational engagement strategy—the stay interview? We asked colleagues, book reviewers, and clients around the globe and here is what we heard.

- The majority said, "It will work here just as well as in the United States."

- One colleague said, "Barriers to 'asking' in Asia are magnified because the culture demands respect for elders and leaders. Even if asked, most employees do not feel free to share issues that may reflect negatively on their boss."

- A Chinese proverb reads, "A man of honor will feel ashamed by a single question to which he does not know the answer."

- A consultant reported, "In more hierarchical cultures like that of Japan and Korea, asking questions is not traditionally encouraged. If the boss were to say, 'What do you think?' the subordinate would say, 'Yes.'"

If you manage others in a culture where asking is not accepted or recommended, you'll need to find a work-around. Some managers have used anonymous surveys or tasked someone else with the "asking." However you seek to learn about what your talented employees really want, it is crucial that you do gain that information.

To Do

★ Look back at the list of reasons people stay and ask yourself which of these you can influence.

★ Check all those that you believe are largely within your control. If our hunch is correct, you will find that you can influence many more than you may have thought.

Beyond "Why Did You Stay?"

For a decade now, we've collected managers' favorite stay interview questions. Here are the top 13.

Stay Interview Questions

1. What about your job makes you jump out of bed in the morning?

2. What makes you hit the snooze button?

3. If you were to win the lottery and resign, what would you miss the most about your job?

4. What one change in your current role would make you consider leaving this job?

5. If you had a magic wand, what would be the one thing you would change about this department, team, organization?

6. As your manager, what could I do a little more of or a little less of?

7. If you had to go back to a position in your past and stay for an extended period of time, which one would it be and why?

8. What do you need to learn to work at your best?

9. What makes for a great day?

10. What can we do to make your job more satisfying?

11. What can we do to support your career goals?

12. Do you get enough recognition? How do you like to be recognized?

13. What do you want to learn this year?

Let these ideas serve as catalysts for your own thinking. Create a list of your favorite questions. Ask them of your talented people. And ask again, listen carefully, and customize your retention efforts.

Bottom Line

Stop guessing what will keep your stars happy and on your team. Gather your courage and conduct stay interviews with the employees you want to keep. Set aside time to start the dialogue. Don't guess and don't assume they all want the same thing (like pay or promotion). Schedule another meeting if they need to think about it for a while.

To simply *ask* may be the most important strategy in this book. Not only will asking make your talented people feel valued, but their answers will provide the information you need to customize strategies to keep each of them.

It doesn't matter so much where, when, or how you ask—just ASK!

TWO

Buck
IT STOPS HERE

*Ponder this: Who's really in charge of engaging
and retaining your best people?*

This sign was on President Truman's White House office desk, and Truman popularized the now-familiar phrase. Every culture has its way of saying do not pass the buck. In Chinese it goes like this, 责无旁贷, and it translates to "No shirking of responsibility."

When we ask supervisors and managers how to keep good people, many immediately respond, "With money." Research suggests that a majority of managers truly believe it's largely about the money. These managers place the responsibility for keeping key people squarely in the hands of senior management. They blame organizational policies or pay scales for the loss of talent. Or they point the finger at the competition or the location. It's always someone else's fault.

Well, the truth is, *you matter most.* If you are a manager at any level, a front-line supervisor, or a project leader, you actually have more power than anyone else to keep your best employees. Why? Because the factors that drive employee satisfaction, engagement, and commitment are largely within your control. And the factors that satisfy and engage employees are the ones that keep them on your team. Those factors haven't changed much over the past 25 years. Many researchers who have studied retention agree on what engages or satisfies people and therefore influences them to stay: meaningful and challenging work, a chance to learn and grow, fair and competitive compensation, great coworkers, recognition, respect, and a good boss. Don't you want those things?

Alas *There's nothing I can do about our brain drain. The competition is offering more money and better perks. We don't stand a chance.*

—Manager, retail pharmacy

You *do* stand a chance. Your relationship with employees is key to their satisfaction and decisions to stay or leave. Consider this:

- Research by the Gallup Organization found that at least 75 percent of the reasons for voluntary turnover can be influenced by managers.[2]

- Watson Wyatt reported that the relationship with the supervisor/manager was the top-ranked reason employers gave for why employees leave an organization, cited by 31 percent of respondents.[3]

- A Conference Board consolidation of 12 major studies on employee engagement found that all studies agreed that the relationship with one's manager was the strongest drive of all.[4]

- A Center for Creative Leadership/Booz Allen Hamilton study found that among those who strongly agreed that they work for a manager who cares about their well-being, 94 percent said they intend to stay with their current employer. Of those who strongly disagreed that their manager cared about their well-being, just 43 percent planned to stick around.[5]

- Research by the authors (over 18,000 respondents) found that most retention factors are within managers' influence.

The evidence is clear. The buck stops with the manager. That reality is taking hold in organizations across the globe. Managers who think engagement and retention are somebody else's job need to think again.

In our exit interviews, for those who are honest, the major reason people leave is conflict with their manager. That needs to be dealt with, and those relationships need to be strengthened. Most managers do not see creating a retention culture as their responsibility. They do need to own this responsibility and be held accountable to create and maintain this culture.

—*CEO, nonprofit firm in Singapore*

It's Up to You

Be a love 'em manager. A good boss who cares about keeping good employees will help them find what they want from their workplace. We're not saying you carry this responsibility alone. Senior management and your organization's policies, systems, and culture have an impact on your ability to keep talented people. You may have human resource professionals who can help support your efforts. Even your employees have a role. (See our book *Love It, Don't Leave It: 26 Ways to Get What You Want at Work*.)

Yet, because of what research tells us about *why* people leave their jobs and organizations, you still have the greatest power (and responsibility) for keeping your talented employees.

"Bosses matter to everyone they oversee, but they matter most to those just beneath them in the pecking order: the people they guide at close range, who constantly tangle with the boss's virtues, foibles, and quirks. Whether you are the CEO of a Fortune 500 company or the head chef at a restaurant, your success depends on staying in tune with the people you interact with most frequently and intensely."

Linda Hudson, CEO of BAE Systems, got this message after becoming the first female president of General Dynamics. After her first day on the job, a dozen women in her office imitated how she tied her scarf. Hudson realized, "It really was now about me and the context of setting the tone for the organization. That was a lesson I have never forgotten—that as a leader, people are looking at you in a way that you could not have imagined in other roles." Hudson added that such scrutiny and the consequent responsibility is "something that I think about virtually every day."[6]

To Do

★ Start with a conversation—a "stay interview." Learn about your talented employees' goals and what they love (or don't love) about their work. Don't stop with one chat. Talk (and listen!) daily, weekly, monthly. Develop a true relationship with every single person you hope to keep on your team.

★ Hold "Alas Clinics"—opportunities to talk with others about talented people who have left your team lately. Why did they go? What role (if any) did you play in their leaving? How can you prevent more unwanted turnover?

★ Think about who might be "loose in the saddle" (about ready to leave you); talk with them *soon,* and collaborate with them to get more of what they want and need from you, from the team, from their jobs.

★ Go big picture. Ask yourself, "What kind of work environment do I want to create?" Then figure out what you need to do in order to make that vision come alive. Then—go do it!

GO TO

Numbers
page 131

So They Go

So what? Can't you just replace them? You might be able to replace your key people, but at what cost? Most retention experts agree that replacing key talent will cost you two times their annual salaries. And replacing "platinum" workers (those with specialized skills) will run four to five times their annual salary.

Even if you can afford to replace them, will you be able to find skilled replacements?

You think 1999 was a bad time to be hiring? That year was only a footprint for what we'll see in the future. We'll be facing the worst labor shortage in our lifetime within the next five years.

—Jeff Taylor, founder, Monster

The demographers and workforce pundits disagree. Will we be short millions of workers in the coming decades or have plenty to go around? The mitigating factors to talent shortages (globalization/offshoring, technology advances, delayed retirement, immigration) are so many and so complex that some feel a crystal ball would do as good a job as the experts when it comes to projecting the answer.

What we do know is this: the labor market is changing, and in many segments there aren't enough *skilled* workers to fill the jobs open today, let alone support a growing economy. Notice what's happening in your own backyard. Do you have plenty of people, with exactly the right skills, to step in when you lose a key contributor? Or is there a current or pending talent shortage in your industry, geography, or job function?

On the Line

Most of you are in charge of certain assets. You are held accountable for protecting those assets and for growing them. Today, your most critical assets are *people,* not property. Outstanding people give you and your organization a competitive advantage. Regardless of the job market, you no doubt want to hold on to your best.

Are you accountable for selecting and keeping talented people? We have heard of a CEO who charged $30,000 to a manager's operating budget because he needlessly lost a talented person. The buck really did stop there!

We're not suggesting that managers be punished when their people are promoted or move on to learn something new. You will inevitably lose some talented employees occasionally, especially as they pursue their career dreams. But we do recommend that managers be held accountable for being *good managers* and for creating a retention culture where people feel motivated, cared about, and rewarded.

Bottom Line

The retention buck really does stop with you. We are not ignoring the impact of senior management, organization policies, and individual employees' attitudes and actions. But we know you have great power to influence your talented employees' decisions about staying. Conduct stay interviews with every employee you hope to engage and keep on your team. Find out what they want and help them get it! Show that you care about them and their needs. Remember them. Notice them. Listen to them. Thank them. Love them or lose them.

THREE

Careers
SUPPORT GROWTH

Ponder this: Are you helping build their future,
or are you in the way?

Our research and that of many others around the globe consistently find that having career opportunities is one of the primary reasons people stay and *produce*.

> *In Asia, you must provide career opportunities to grow or your talent will walk away. People will leave corporations they do not feel aligned with. Compensation is not always the driving force. Development opportunities are.*
> —Member of Asia-Pacific Talent and
> Diversity Council, Conference Board

Yet, far too many managers steer clear of career conversations. They worry about opening a Pandora's box. If these leaders fail to have ongoing chats with their talented people, they stand a far greater chance of losing them—either physically or psychologically.

Which of the following barriers keep *you* from opening up this topic?

- No one, let alone me, knows what the future holds.

- It is just not the right time.

- I'm not prepared.

- I wouldn't know what to say.

- We've just reorganized. It will be a while before anyone knows anything about career possibilities.

- I would never open something I couldn't close.

- I don't know enough about what's outside my department to offer advice.

- I don't want anyone blaming me if they don't get what they want.

- Why should I help? Nobody ever helped me.

What your employees really want are two-way conversations with you to talk about their abilities, choices, and ideas. They want you to listen. They may not expect you to have the answers, but they expect and really want to have the dialogue.

Talking to your employees about their careers does take time and may seem like a tough assignment. You may want to start with employees who have expressed concern about their careers or with employees who show signs of becoming disengaged from their work. Prioritize and take one step at a time. Your efforts will pay off in productivity and retention.

What if you thought about career conversations as one of the perks of your job?

When I look at the wonderful people who work with me in my department, and the many, many talents they possess, I can do nothing short of helping them become better and better. I am privileged to be in a position to encourage their growth . . . and when they grow, I feel blessed that I somehow played a small part.

—Director, Surgical Services for a major health care firm

Five steps you can take routinely will build your talent pipeline and support your employees' search for a good career fit.[7]

Step 1: Know their talents.

Step 2: Offer your perspective.

Step 3: Discuss trends.

Step 4: Discover multiple options.

Step 5: Codesign an action plan.

Step 1: Know Their Talents

The primary objective of career conversations is to gather information that will tell you more about your employees. It is not always easy for them to talk about their skills, values, and interests. Some will think of it as bragging, or they'll fear appearing disloyal if they discuss career goals beyond the current job. (Many managers in Asia report this to be a challenge—how to hold an honest career discussion, given cultural norms and values that support humility and loyalty.)

The ultimate goal is to ask questions about your employees' unique skills, interests, and values. The toughest part is to listen while they answer, as a diligent researcher would. Probe, inquire, and discover more.

GO TO
___
Understand
page 206

To Do

Try asking these questions, and then probe each answer more deeply:

★ What makes you unique in this organization?

★ Tell me about one of your accomplishments that makes you particularly proud.

★ What are your most important work-related values? Which values are met and not met at work?

★ If you had to choose among working with people, data, things, or ideas, which mixture would be most satisfying? Why?

Get curious. Ask good probing questions (avoiding ones that give you only yes or no answers), and you'll gain a deeper understanding of what really matters to your employees. Be patient with people who've never had a boss ask these kinds of questions and might be uncomfortable responding initially.

Step 2: Offer Your Perspective

Help your employees reflect on their own reputations, on the feedback they've gotten from others, and on the areas they need to develop. And give them honest feedback regularly.

GO TO

Truth
page 196

Think back to the last performance review you gave. It probably was based on past performance and connected to that employee's raise. Development feedback is different. It is future oriented and focuses on areas where the employee can improve.

Employees want specific feedback with examples of their performance and the effect on their future goals. Have them seek out colleagues at all levels who will give them a more realistic self-portrait to help them develop faster and smarter. And remember—development feedback includes good news as well as corrective input!

To Do

Include these questions in your conversation:

★ What is the most helpful feedback you have received? How did it change your behavior? How did you apply that to your work?

★ In which areas do you wish I would give you more feedback? How can I help you feel more accomplished and successful at work?

★ Which of your team skills are most valued by your colleagues? How do you know? Based on their feedback, which skills do you hope to improve?

Think about all the awkward conversations you've had with employees whose career goals are simply out of sync with reality given their strengths and weaknesses. Our hunch is that *the absence of honest feedback kept them out of sync.* Employees continually tell us that they want straight talk. Want to keep them? Level with them.

Step 3: Discuss Trends

Help your employees consider their options by encouraging them to look beyond your department, to detect shifts and changes that might impact their careers. Think about your company's growth areas and limitations as well as emerging skills the industry will require. Share this information with your employees. Helping your employees see what's down the road is a sign of respect, even if it isn't all good news.

Alas

Lenore was exactly what our organization needed. She was young and wanted to use her technical as well as managerial skills, wanted to develop business, and in fact had already brought some in. She decided to look for a new job when she heard that there were some changes coming in our organization, and she realized she didn't know what would happen to her. She said that her first manager was great at coaching and keeping her in the loop, but that she had recently been moved to work for another manager who had shown no interest in her career. So with the threat of impending change, and a manager who didn't seem to care, she took an offer at a small start-up company. She was clear that it was not the salary and benefits that drew her. It was the hope of a better manager, one who would keep her "in the loop" and care about her career. The exit interview lasted 90 minutes. I asked her if she would reconsider. She declined.

—Human resources manager

Clearly, a good career conversation with her new manager could have influenced Lenore's decision to look for other opportunities.

To Do

Ask yourself if your employees know what the trends are in these areas:

★ The major economic, political, technological and social changes taking place that will have the greatest effect on your organization

★ The opportunities and problems ahead

★ The areas changing the most in your industry

★ How their profession will be different in the next two to five years

★ What really counts for success in your organization

★ Which websites, trade publications, journals, and organization newsletters provide information on industry and business trends

★ What new opportunities are available (e.g., international assignments, new businesses opening within the organization)

You don't have to take this all on your own shoulders. For example, you could have each person on your team research one of these areas and bring it to the next staff meeting for discussion. But you do have to ensure that your employees know what's going on in your organization. By suggesting others who can provide additional perspectives on these and other issues, you open channels for your employees and give them a closer look at the key business needs of the organization. Have you done this lately?

GO TO
_____

Goals
page 53

Step 4: Discover Multiple Options

Help your employees consider multiple career goals while they grow within their current positions. When employees analyze their potential development goals in terms of business needs and the strategic intent of the organization, everyone wins.

Caution! The employee is still primarily responsible for his or her career. Our suggestions do not mean *telling* the person what to do. Instead, offer choices for employees to analyze and consider.

Offering choices is important, but sometimes difficult. For generations, the only acceptable career direction has been up. (Actually, that is still often true in many cultures and companies.) But there are at least five other ways employees can move their careers along. You can help your employees consider options like these:

- Move laterally (a change in job, but not necessarily a change in the level of responsibility)

- Explore (requires answering questions like "What else can I do?")

- Enrich (seeds the current job with more chances to learn and grow)

- Realign (reconciles the demands of work with other priorities, or readies them for another area)

- Relocate (yes, leaving the organization if the work simply cannot match a person's skills, interests, or values)

You can give your employees permission to discover the possibilities based on their interests, what they value, and what they can contribute to the organization.

The more options your employee identifies, the better. Exits and disengagements occur when an employee's only goal is thwarted.

To Do

Help your employees answer these challenging questions:

★ Do you have enough information about the organization's current activities and plans to select several career goals?

★ How can you get the information you need?

★ Have you considered all available directions in selecting your career options?

★ Do your options adequately cover a variety of scenarios?

★ Should you select more career options?

★ Are your goals compatible with organizational goals and plans?

Once you have helped your employees look at options so that not all of their plans reflect the vertical mindset, they will feel as if they have more leverage to manage their own careers.

Step 5: Codesign an Action Plan

Codesigning action steps will increase commitment to a career plan. Consider all of the steps the employee would have to take to realize the best career goals, and then develop contingency plans for each. Then, if one is blocked, you already will have laid out other paths together.

Help your employees identify the obstacles to each path. Then brainstorm ways around the obstacles. During the process, help them to remember and maximize the assets they already have.

Leaders will have to learn what the successful conductors of the symphony orchestra have long known: The key to greatness is to look for people's potential and spend time developing it.[8]

To Do

Try asking any or all of these questions. The answers form the action plan.

★ What skills would you need to gain to help you achieve your goals?

★ What abilities do you already have that would help you toward any of your goals?

★ Who is in your network already who might open a door for you?

★ What training could I make available to fill the gaps you see?

★ What kinds of on-the-job development could help you move closer to several of your options?

Remember, your job is to help your employees identify the skills, development opportunities, and knowledge areas required for each alternative. Your job is not to build their plans but to support them.

Bottom Line

Employees have one thing in common: they want to know that someone cares about their careers. And that someone should be you if you want engaged, productive people on your team. Help them find opportunities to sculpt their careers according to their own unique wants and needs. When you do this, you'll find your best employees will want to stay a while and build their careers in *your* organization.

FOUR

SHOW RESPECT

Ponder this: In how many ways do you show you respect them?

What kind of boss would your employees say you are? Would they say that you are smart, dedicated, motivating, hard-charging? How about results oriented, demanding, or fun to work with? Just as you tolerate a range of behaviors from your employees, so, too, your employees will accept you as you are, no doubt less than perfect but doing your best.

The one behavior that talented people seldom tolerate for long is disrespect. If you wish to keep them, it is absolutely critical that you recognize each person's unique qualities and then demonstrate your respect in consistent, undeniable ways.

Alas

We lost one of our most important paralegal assistants. Every attorney in our office counted on her, and we were shocked to see her go. In her exit interview, she said it was not the pay or perks that caused her to seek a new job. It was the daily and weekly indignities that she suffered while trying to do her best in this job. Her performance review (and possible raise) had been overlooked for the past six months. Her request to join an association of paralegals still lay on her boss's desk after six weeks. She was denied attendance at a free seminar that would have benefited the firm, because they couldn't free her up. She had not been thanked for her hard work and excellent results. Her boss grunted and vented and took out his frustrations on her without giving it a second thought. She finally left the firm because she did not feel respected or valued, but she did feel used and demeaned. And everyone noticed.

—Attorney, major law firm

Could that happen at your workplace? Have you, or has someone you know (even one of your direct reports), ever left for reasons like that?

Respect—in any Language

You cannot respect and honor others unless you respect—even celebrate—the differences between people. Can you imagine how ineffective (and boring) your team would be if everyone thought the same, looked the same, believed the same, had the same talents? Most of us readily accept the notion that diversity of talent and perspective strengthens a work group and contributes to excellent results. Yet if we are honest, we admit that differences also get in the way. The hard truth is that many of us more often tolerate than celebrate differences.

The Museum of Tolerance in Los Angeles welcomes its visitors in a unique way. As tour groups form in the lobby, they are invited into a waiting room that admits them into the museum. Our tour guide said to us, "Notice that there are two doors through which you may enter this museum. One is marked 'prejudiced' and the other is marked 'unprejudiced.' You may enter through whichever door represents you." There was a long pause as people pondered what they should do, which door to choose. Finally, a man bravely stepped forward and turned the knob on the door marked "unprejudiced." A few stepped forward to follow him, while the rest of us watched. He turned the knob, looked a little confused, and then turned red with embarrassment as he realized the door was locked. We could only enter the museum through the door marked "prejudiced."

—*Sharon Jordan-Evans*

Which door would you have chosen? How would you react to the locked door? We all need to take a good look at our preferences and prejudices, our *leanings*. We all have them. They pop up when we mentor and coach, promote, reward, punish, and hire (research shows we are most apt to hire someone like ourselves). Once you take note of your leanings, you can begin to see the impact they might have on your employees.

Museum of Tolerance designers assumed that we all carry prejudices. The issue is how we respond. The first step in leveraging differences is to take a good look at your own beliefs. How much do you respect people who are very different from yourself? Do you value what they bring to your team? How sincerely do you want them to stay?

Managers must have multinational skills. They will have to work shoulder to shoulder with people from many nationalities in the global village of the twenty-first century. They must understand them, speak to them, cooperate with them, manage them effectively, not lose out to them, yet like and praise them. These are our cultural challenges.

— *Richard Lewis, author of* When Cultures
Collide: Leading Across Cultures

To Do

★ Analyze your perspective. Admit to your leanings toward or away from those with different

- Skin color

- Status

- Education

- Height or weight

- Title

- Accent

- Geographic origin

- Learning style

- Personality

- Management status

- Religion

- Educational background

- Union affiliation

- Work habits

- Age

- Job function

- Gender

- Lifestyle

- Sexual orientation

- Talent

- _____ (add one)

- _____ (add one)

★ Add to the list. What do you tend to lean toward or away from?

★ Notice how your _leanings_ play out at work. Whom did you last promote? Whom do you tend to ignore, praise less often, and be less friendly with? Whom do you really _listen_ to most often?

★ Learn about the differences among your employees. To accomplish this, one manager held a discovery day, where people were encouraged to talk about themselves, how they grew up, the holidays they observe, and why.

★ Leverage the differences. Roosevelt Thomas, a diversity consultant and author, defines diversity as "the maximum utilization of talent in the workforce."[9] Appreciate and use individual strengths, styles, and talents.

★ *Decide* to change. Practice inclusion and fairness. Consciously avoid discriminating in the old familiar ways. Your employees will notice.

When people get their backs up about diversity, often they're resisting what they see as an effort to change how they feel. Valuing differences does not force you to change how you feel. It may persuade you to change how you act at work to keep good employees.

Remember that there is no genetic predisposition to bias; no bias gene rides on your chromosomes; no DNA test can identify who is biased and who is not. Bias is learned. It's an acquired habit of thought rooted in fear and fueled by conditioning and, as such, can be unacquired and deconditioned. That's good news because no one can afford to allow his or her distorted vision to interfere with the ability to function effectively, fairly, and successfully in increasingly diverse workplaces.

—*Sondra Thiederman*

Manage Your Sloppy Moods

Honoring others and treating them with dignity and respect may mean managing your moods. Have you ever worked for someone with roller-coaster moods? You know, one day she's up; the next she's *way* down. While it is human to have ups and downs, it is grown-up to manage those moods so that they do not hurt others. Some call moods that have run amok *sloppy moods.* They are simply uncontrolled. Whatever is felt comes spilling out and

GO TO

Jerk
page 86

slops all over employees (or family). The results can be embarrassment, hurt, anger, humiliation, and loss of dignity.

To Do

★ If you are guilty of sloppy moods, take notice and take control. Get away from others while you work through your difficulties. Go to your room; take a *time-out*.

★ If you happen to slop on someone, apologize. To err is human, and most people appreciate an apology; it is a sign of respect.

★ If you have a serious problem managing your moods, consider seeking help from a professional or your organization's Employee Assistance Program (EAP).

Meanness is so last millennium. Niceness is the future.[10]

Are They Invisible?

My previous boss never said hello to me. He would walk right past me in the hall as if I did not exist, or was invisible. He did say hello to every vice president. My new boss treats me with respect. I feel like she values me as a person, even though her job level is above mine. I love working here.

—*Bank teller*

When employees talk about the disrespect that drove them out the door to a new job, they sometimes refer to this feeling of invisibility. You might be simply lost in thought when you pass your employees in the hall and fail to acknowledge them. But they will notice and may feel less than honored or respected.

Note: Different cultures show respect differently. Our Asian colleagues say that while respect is key, bosses may not be likely to smile or greet their employees in the hallway; it's just not part of the cultural norm. They also say that the bosses who *do* smile and say hello are sure to win over their people!

To Do

★ Notice your employees. Pay attention as you walk down the halls and say hello to them by name.

★ Smile, shake hands, greet your employees, and introduce them to others, even those of higher rank. They will feel honored and definitely not invisible.

Trust Me

Some say that trust is a gift. Others say it must be earned. Still others refuse to trust anyone at all. Andy Grove, chairman of Intel, even wrote a book called *Only the Paranoid Survive.* Great title, but in practice it is a tough way to live!

What we know is that when you trust your employees, most will be trustworthy. They will feel honored and respected when you trust them with important tasks and heavy responsibilities and when you let them do things their way. When you fail to trust them, they will often feel dishonored, disrespected, and undervalued. And you can bet they will leave when a better opportunity presents itself.

If you doubt this, think about a time in your career when you had a boss who trusted you implicitly, trusted you to excel, trusted you with information or assets. How did you feel? How committed did you feel to the boss or the organization as a result?

He simply could not learn to trust us. It was as if he thought we were all out to get him, and in the end it was almost a self-fulfilling prophecy. We knew we were worthy of his trust, and yet we almost began to feel guilty as he micromanaged us and constantly looked over our shoulders. We had to account for every minute of our time and every nickel we spent. Finally, it was just too demeaning. The entire team decided to find other employment and a boss who trusted us.

—Director, engineering firm

If only the boss had trusted his team. They were truly not out to get him—they were just trying to do their jobs. To trust someone implicitly shows tremendous respect for that person.

Nine out of ten employees say that true success is about being trusted to get the job done.[11]

To Do

★ Check out your own ability to trust others. Do you tend to offer trust as a gift or demand evidence of trustworthiness before you give it?

★ Try trusting your employees. Say you trust them, act like you trust them, and *really* trust them. Give them responsibility and then let them carry it out.

What's Fair Is Fair

Talented workers will leave a boss who is perceived to be unfair. Unfair treatment translates to disrespect in many employees' minds. Check out your communication approach and your actions with your employees. How do they view the decisions and changes that you make? What seems fair or unfair to them? Do you honor their ideas, and do you care about their reactions? If you don't, you will lose them.

Always do what is right. It will gratify most of the people, and astound the rest.

—*Mark Twain*

Anybody Home?

Sometimes busy bosses seem almost unreachable. Unless the sky is falling (by their definition), it is virtually impossible to get their attention. An employee wants to leave early on Friday for his son's baseball game and asks you on the Monday before. Another employee needs your okay to attend a conference in two months. A third employee's wife has been hospitalized with a life-threatening illness. What do you do? Ideally you respond quickly in all three cases.

Unfortunately, too many busy bosses tell the first and second employees that they will get back to them but never do. The employees feel unimportant and disrespected and have to either nag for an answer or forget the whole thing (but they never really do). And what does the busy boss do about the third employee? Too often: nothing. Treating an employee with dignity means acknowledging how difficult and unique this life situation is.

My mother was dying of cancer and lived 1,000 miles away. I was a wreck at work, unable to concentrate, and feeling so guilty about not being with her. My boss took me into his office and told me to take as much time as I needed to go and be with my mother in her final days. I will never forget that act. I felt so valued and respected by him that my commitment to the organization soared.

—*Secretary, consulting firm*

To Do

★ Listen to your employees' wants and needs. Even concerns that seem small or insignificant are clearly important to them.

★ Respond to their requests quickly. Don't wait for them to nag you.

★ Be aware and take steps to help employees in their times of need. They will pay you back a thousand-fold.

Bottom Line

Respecting others may seem easy enough. After all, it's really just an attitude, isn't it? Attitudes and beliefs are at the core of showing respect and honoring others. But behaviors and actions are involved, too. Check out your beliefs about differences, and audit your actions. Listen to your employees, respond to them, and—bottom line—treat them with respect and dignity.

FIVE

ENERGIZE THE JOB

*Ponder this: Do your people have to leave
to learn something new?*

Our favorite "stay interview" question is "What do you want to learn this year?" It seems all great performers are interested in learning. And when promotions and pay raises are in short supply, you might turn to learning as a way to enrich their jobs, alleviate boredom, even re-recruit them to your team and to your purpose. Learning on the job is a powerful way to engage or reengage with the work.

It Can Happen to Anyone

Did your own "job EKG" ever go flat? Did the feeling of challenge change to a feeling of routine? Did you think something was missing? What happened to your energy? In any case, did you start to wonder what else there was? Did you start to look around?

Unfortunately, your most valued employees are the most likely to suffer this sense of job discontent. By definition, they are savvy, creative, self-propelled, and energetic. They need stimulating work, opportunities for personal challenge and growth, and a contributing stake in the organizational action.

If good workers find that your company no longer provides these necessities, they may decide they have outgrown the place and will consider leaving, or worse yet, disengage on the job. If they disengage, their departure is psychological rather than physical. It shows up in absenteeism and mediocre performance. These people simply withhold their energy and effort, figuring, "What's the point, anyway?"

Either way, through departure or disengagement, you lose talented people who are vital to the success of your unit and your company—a preventable loss.

Alas

I had been doing the same work for seven years when my organization decided to expand the business in a new direction. I met with my boss to tell him that I would love to learn about the new side of the business and maybe expand my job to include at least some work in the new arena. I wasn't sure how it could all fit, but I knew I wanted something new and exciting in my day-to-day work life. When I raised the topic, he responded curtly, "The team has already been chosen to do this new work. We need you to keep doing what you're doing." That was the end of our discussion. I left the organization six months later.

—Claims adjuster, insurance company

Get Enriched Quick

Job enrichment means a change in what your employees do (content) or how they do it (process) and it inevitably involves learning. Enrichment helps employees to find the growth, challenge, and renewal they seek without leaving their current jobs or employers.

An enriched job is composed of one or more of these features:

- Gives employees room to initiate, create, and implement new ideas

- Promotes setting and achieving personal and group goals

- Allows employees to see their contributions to an end product or goal

- Challenges employees to expand their knowledge and capabilities

- Allows employees to "job sculpt" and make the job they have a job they love

A job can be as neatly tailored to a worker's peculiar goals and requirements as a pair of Levi's [jeans] to an online customer's imperfect physique.

—David Ulrich and David Sturm

If enrichment is so beneficial, why isn't it a standard part of every job? One good reason is this: what enriches one employee is different from what enriches the next. Courtney, devastated by her job's predictability, craves variety in each day's tasks. Marcos, tired of being told how to do his audit reports, is ready to teach someone else how to do them. Sofia sees that her computer programs meet the needs of her superiors and now wants to spend more time creating useful applications for her colleagues. How do you tailor job enrichment to individuals and their needs? Ask them what would enrich their jobs! (Duh.)

GO TO

Ask
page 1

To Do

Use these questions to help people probe for possibilities of enrichment:

★ In what ways is your job important to the company?

★ What skills do you use on the job? What talents and interests do you have that you don't use?

★ What about your job do you find challenging or rewarding? What's not challenging or rewarding about your job?

★ In what areas would you like increased responsibility for your current tasks?

★ What would you like to be doing in the next three to five years?

★ In what ways would you like your job changed?

Ask these questions to help people evaluate their jobs and discover ideas for enrichment. Their responses will, and should, vary greatly from person to person.

The Learning Assignment

We said that learning is core to enrichment. Now let's look at how a learning assignment brought back the "juice" of the job for one employee.

When Sergey's boss asked what he wanted to learn next year, he said, "I'd like to improve my negotiating skills." The boss said, "Great, let's do it," and they began a three-step learning process. Here are the steps they followed and how it worked out for Sergey.

Step 1. Conscious Observation. *Sergey's boss selected an expert for Sergey to observe—someone who was exceptionally skilled at negotiating. After the observation, Sergey and his boss discussed what Sergey noticed, learned, would mirror or do differently.*

Step 2. Selected Participation. *Sergey's boss gave him the chance to take a well-defined but limited role in a negotiation (preparing the opening re-marks with a vendor). The goal was to give Sergey an opportunity to get his feet wet without feeling overwhelmed. Following the meeting, Sergey and his boss discussed what worked and where there might be room for improvement.*

Step 3. Key Responsibility. *Sergey's boss gave him primary responsibility for a project that required excellent negotiation skills. Sergey completed the entire negotiation with the vendor and was both visible and accountable for the outcome. His boss was present, of course, but would have stepped in only if Sergey requested his support.*

It worked. One year later, Sergey is thrilled with his job and continues to de-velop mastery as a negotiator for his organization.

Note: Any one of these steps can be the learning assignment, in and of itself.

Consider the Possibilities

The bedrock of most enrichment activities is learning. Yet, enrichment can take on many different forms. Remember to ask your talented employees what they'd like to do and how they'd like to do it. Here are some techniques that work if you are careful to match them to individual wants and needs:

- *Form teams.* Self-directed work groups can make a lot of their own de-cisions. They can redistribute work so that team members learn more, have more variety, and follow more projects through to completion.

- *Touch the client.* For example, a computer systems troubleshooter might be more effective knowing the needs of real people and units rather than responding only to problems as they occur. Assign one troubleshooter to one department (the client), and make her accountable for that cli-ent's success in using the company's computer system. It's amazing how many employees never see their clients.

- **_Rotate assignments._** New responsibilities can help an employee feel challenged and valued. Employees can acquire important new skills that add depth to the workforce. Do rotational assignments sound like chaos? Suggest the idea and let your employees propose the "who" and "how" part; you'll be surprised at their expertise in making it happen smoothly.

- **_Increase feedback._** Do more than annual reviews. Find ways to develop peer review and client review opportunities. Employees want to know about their performance, and continual feedback allows them to be their own quality control agents.

- **_Involve employees in decisions._** Employees are empowered and motivated when they take part in decisions that have an impact on their work, such as budget and hiring decisions, or ways to organize work and schedules. Involvement allows employees to see the big picture and enables them to make a contribution they find meaningful.

- **_Nurture creativity._** Untapped creativity dwindles. If employees rarely think for themselves, they lose the ability to contribute their best ideas. They simply go through the paces, undermotivated and disengaged. You can help by asking for and rewarding creative ideas, by giving employees the freedom and resources to create, and by challenging employees with new assignments, tasks, and learning.

- **_Teach someone._** Teaching another person is motivational for many. If an employee has a particular niche or specialty and enjoys passing this knowledge on, you have a perfect win-win!

- **_Support enrollment in learning opportunities._** German law provides for a _Bildungsurlaub_, five days off per year to participate in an approved training course. Training doesn't have to be directly connected to a job as long as it is approved by the state. Although not many countries have a law like this, the idea of enriching a job via a learning experience is something any manager in any organization can explore.

To Do

Give these job enrichment ideas to your employees. Ask them to add to the list and to get specific about the enrichment goals they're considering. Then have them choose two or three favorites. And before they lock on to their goals for the coming weeks or months, make sure they complete the Payoff Potential Quiz here. Better yet, discuss the questions with them. Their answers to the quiz will help them decide which goals to pursue next.

Payoff Potential Quiz

If you choose this enrichment goal . . .

- What's in it for you?
  - ★ How will it build your skills?
  - ★ How will it increase your marketability in your organization? In your profession?
  - ★ How will it increase your reputation as a specialist or generalist?
  - ★ How will it help you gain more confidence and competence in your current position?
  - ★ How will it extend your network?
  - ★ How will it spice up your day-to-day work life?
- What's in it for your work group?
  - ★ How will it help you work more effectively with your current team?
  - ★ How will it increase/enhance your contribution to your work group or department?
  - ★ How will it make their lives better, easier, more fun?
- What's in it for the organization?
  - ★ How will it increase your value to the organization?

* How does it contribute to current organizational mission, strategy, or goals?

* How does it address a current relevant business need?

Note: The "What's in It for You?" section is first and longest. That's on purpose!

As you think about job enrichment, don't feel as if you have to have all the answers, and don't let yourself become the "fix-it" person. This is a collaborative process between you and every one of the talented people on your team. Ultimately, your employees need to move the needle on their own job satisfaction—with your support, of course! We wrote a book to help them do just that. It's called *Love It, Don't Leave It: 26 Ways to Get What You Want at Work*.

Bottom Line

If you help employees enrich their jobs, you can benefit them, their teams, and the entire organization. Stay alert to enrichment opportunities for all your employees. Encourage them to suggest ways to enrich their own jobs. Watch their "job EKGs" spike!

SIX

GET FRIENDLY

Ponder this: Do your employees have to choose
between work and family?

People disengage or quit when rigid workplace rules cause unbearable family stress. Would they leave your organization over work/family conflicts? Yes. Business magazines have spent plenty of ink in recent years on the importance of developing a "family-friendly culture." But what does it really mean?

Employees are asking for a workplace that helps them balance the demands of their work and family lives, rather than forcing them to choose one over the other. Today and from now on, organizations that are not family-friendly will definitely have a harder time finding and keeping good people.

Talented employees do not have to look far to find family-friendly employers who offer features like these:

- Childcare facilities or subsidies

- Flexible work schedules

- Job sharing

- Telecommuting

- Eldercare assistance (such as referral programs)

- Extended and creative maternity or paternity leave programs

Savvy employers give talented employees flexibility in how they work, when they work, and often where they work. They allow employees to meet personal responsibilities while still being productive at work.

If your organization does have these policies and perks in place, that's great. But if not, you have two options. One is to benchmark. Get smart about what other organizations are offering, and then go to your manager (or the human resources department) with information and suggestions. See if you can get some of these ideas adopted in your organization.

Whether or not you take the first option, you can take the more urgent one: become a more family-friendly manager. Start by modeling the behaviors you hope to see. One CEO told his staff that he wouldn't start meetings before 9 a.m. because he takes a daily walk with his wife. He sent a loud message to his management team that it is acceptable, even desirable, to balance family with business goals.

There are many things that you can do to support your employees' lives outside work. The result will be more productive workers who are less likely to stray.

What Does Family Mean, and What Do They Want?

What do we mean by the word *family*? It depends. Some of you might immediately picture small children and two parents. Others picture a young newlywed couple, a single male caring for his aging father, or the members of a large extended family. In the United States, the Gen-X-er and his dog could be a family, while in Asia the pet seldom qualifies.

One family-friendly strategy won't meet all of these employees' individual needs. It's critical to consider the different types of families in your group, and then think about (and talk about) the approaches that will work best for each of them. Remember, the most accurate way to get this information quickly is simply to ask your employees.

GO TO

Ask
page 1

To Do

★ Ask your employees questions like this: "What would make your life easier?" In their answers, look for small things that you, their manager, might be able to do to help. Brainstorm with your employees to create some innovative solutions to their work/family challenges.

Get Flexible

You may feel restricted by your organization's lack of family-friendly programs or policies. Yet you have tremendous opportunities to get family-friendly within your own work group. What you do (and fail to do) as a manager can mean so much to your employees as they juggle work and family. And much of what you can do as a manager costs you and your organization little or nothing.

Alas

Ernie was frustrated and exhausted trying to manage his work and family life. His wife also worked, and they had a six-month-old baby. Ernie wanted to partner with his wife in raising their child, so he began to flex his hours a bit to pick up the baby at childcare or take her to the doctor. His productivity and work quality remained high, but his hours dropped (from 55 to 45 a week) and looked somewhat erratic. The boss told Ernie that he simply had to return to his previous schedule—end of discussion. Even though Ernie tried to explain his needs, the boss had no time and no tolerance. Within two months Ernie had found a new job, one with a family-friendly culture and a boss who allowed him flexibility in his schedule.

Ernie's boss lost a valuable employee, one who may be very costly to replace, because he did not take the time to listen and to design a family-friendly work solution with his employee. Rigidity cost him dearly.

Think flexibly the next time an employee asks you for different work hours or time off to help a spouse, parent, or friend. Think about the real costs of saying yes. Will productivity suffer? Will you set a dangerous precedent? Will that employee begin to take advantage of you?

It is more likely that your employees will applaud (maybe silently) your open-mindedness and willingness to help a valued employee in a time of need. Remember to set clear expectations for your employees' results and hold them to those results. Then you will have room to flex when it matters. And that flexing will pay off! A study by the Swiss Federal Institute of Technology showed that the more flexibility you show, the more positive the impact on employee commitment and loyalty.[12]

Get Supportive

Some managers mistakenly think that they should clearly separate themselves from their employees' personal lives. You have much more to gain by showing your interest in their lives outside work.

> *I was so excited about my daughter's singing debut at her high school. She had been taking vocal lessons, she had developed a strong, beautiful voice, and that day was her chance to show it off. She would sing the national anthem (without accompaniment) during the all-school pep rally at 1 p.m. My boss was excited for me and said, "No problem," when I asked him if I could go watch her. But here's the best part. When I returned, with video in hand, he asked me how it went and asked if I would show him the video. It was such a small thing but meant so much to me. I proudly showed him the video and beamed as he praised my daughter. He showed support in so many ways that day.*
>
> *—Receptionist, manufacturing firm*

We have heard about managers who became involved in several appropriate ways. As you read these approaches, think about which ones might work for you and your employees:

- Allowing employees' children to come to work with them occasionally, usually to celebrate a special occasion or because of a special need

- Driving to an employee's house to be with her and her family following a death in the family

- Accompanying employees to their children's ball games and recitals

- Inviting an employee and his or her parents, relatives, or children to lunch

- Allowing well-behaved pets into the workplace

- Staying late after work to help employees work on Halloween costumes for their children

- Researching eldercare alternatives for an employee who needs help with aging parents

- Sending birthday cards or cakes to employees' family members

- Setting up special e-mail and resource areas on the company intranet for employees' children

- Locating resources (the company lawyer) for an employee struggling with the health insurance company

Here is an example of really showing support:

When people ask me why I stayed at my company for 27 years, I tell them this story: When I was pregnant with my first child—he's now 24—I had trouble with my pregnancy and was sent home for bed rest. After two weeks, I couldn't take it anymore and went back to work. The president of the company called me and said, "I am not going to allow you to go back and forth on the subway." He just sent his car in the morning and took me home at night. At that time, I became a lifetime employee of that organization.

—Chairman and CEO, advertising agency

Get Creative

GO TO

Question
page 157

"We've never done that here." "The policies don't support that." "I'd be in trouble with my boss if I allowed that." These are common excuses among managers who don't know their real power or are afraid to test the limits of the family-friendly (or -unfriendly) rules. Sure, there are constraints and policy guidelines in most organizations. And you have to play by those rules to some degree. But often it pays to get creative on behalf of your employees and their needs. Job-sharing is just one example of a creative solution to a challenging situation.

There was no such thing as job sharing in this organization. We have a long history and cemented policies. After the birth of our children, another director and I decided to go to our boss and ask about the possibility of sharing one job. The job was high level and critical to the organization, so at first there was tremendous concern about even trying it. But our boss took a risk and gained approval for a six-month test period. That was 12 years ago, and we have been sharing the job effectively ever since. Our boss's creativity and flexibility allowed us both to balance family and work. We are tremendously grateful and loyal employees.

—Manager, public utility

To Do

Here are some other strategies and solutions that managers have found in collaboration with their employees. Which might work for you?

★ If employees must travel on weekends, offer something in exchange, such as time off during the week or allowing family members to travel with the employee.

★ When your employees travel to areas where they have family or friends, allow them to spend extra time with those people at the beginning or end of the trip.

★ If company policy absolutely prohibits bringing pets to work, consider a picnic in a park where those furry family members are welcome.

★ Give your employees a "floating" day off each year to be used for a special occasion. Or suggest they go home early on their birthdays or anniversaries.

★ Have a party for your team and their families. Invite the kids (or hire sitters for small ones), and go for pizza together.

★ When an employee asks about working from home, really explore that possibility. What are the upsides? Downsides? Get creative about how that might work to benefit both the employee and your team.

★ Consider subsidizing your employees' home Internet service costs. The monthly costs for Internet use are small compared with the productivity you'll get in return. This also allows them to work effectively from home.

The best kind of creativity is collaborative. Remember to brainstorm a list of ideas *with your employees* and be continuously open to new and innovative ways to balance family and work. Tailor and customize your strategies to employees' needs.

Companies that once expected employees to devote themselves single-mindedly to increasing profits and productivity have adjusted their vision (and their vision statements) to accommodate employees' desire and determination to succeed not just at the office, but at home as well. Balance has started to replace obsession as the value driving most companies and most individuals.[13]

Balance by Any Other Name

As the times change, so does the language. Right now, as you read this book, managers might be talking about work/life integration, or blending versus balancing, or something else altogether. No matter how you name it, it's still about finding a way for your treasured, talented people to have both—a great job and a wonderful family life.

Bottom Line

Good employees leave family-unfriendly workplaces.

Do some of these ideas seem extreme to you? If your definition of family-friendly is allowing your employees to accept an occasional personal phone call, it's time to learn what's going on around you. There are positive payoffs for your efforts, including increased loyalty, money saved, and the competitive edge that a loyal and productive workforce will provide. Become a family-friendly manager, and keep your talent on your team.

SEVEN

Goals
EXPAND OPTIONS

Ponder this: Is "up" the only career path they see?
And is "up" in short supply?

You're inundated with goals. You have performance goals for yourself—and for your employees. You (and they) also have life goals, financial goals, athletic goals, spiritual goals, balance goals, maybe even weight loss goals!

Here, we'll be focusing on career-related goals. You've no doubt set goals for your learning, your growth, and your success at work. Have you linked arm in arm with your treasured, talented people to set these kinds of goals—the ones that help them excel and that increase the odds they'll stay with you for a while?

You Want to Move Where?

Do you get a knot in your stomach when a valued employee begins a conversation with one of these phrases?

- I'd like to talk to you about my career.

- I really want to understand what my career options are.

- I'm interested in talking about my next step.

- I don't understand why he got that promotion. I thought I . . . .

- Only a step up makes me feel appreciated.

Feel the knot? It's understandable. You value employees with superb skills who have mastered the current job and want more. They may get calls from recruiters. They want a chance to run the project. They're in your office, looking to you for a much-needed, much-deserved conversation about moving up in the organization. You want to keep them. And "up" is in short supply.

You may lose some of them. However, our 20 years of research reveal that not all those who say they want vertical moves will leave if they don't get them. But they *will* leave (physically or psychologically) if they are not challenged, growing, and having new experiences. So what can you do for them if up is not an option?

Moving Forward Instead of Up

What if your employees began to think about other ways of moving? What if each move challenged and rewarded them? What if they could move forward instead of up?

Sometimes you can prevent turnover by helping your employees identify several career goals. If employees see that you can support several viable alternatives, they will picture a future for themselves within your organization.

I was ready for a promotion, and it looked like there was no place for me at the next level. Then my manager told me about an opportunity to work in the Seattle operation. I jumped at the chance and have been here five years now. Initially the adjustment was tough, but the challenges and growth have been unbelievable—probably even better than had I gotten my sought-after promotion in Dublin.

—*Microsoft programmer from Dublin*

Right Person, Right Place, Right Time

Human resource professionals and managers often repeat this phrase. It's never been easy to achieve. But here's a twist to consider: What if there were more *right* places? Would there not be more *right* times for all those *right* people?

We believe that inside any organization there are four possible moves in addition to moving up. We also believe that the more specifically you can outline those moves, the less likely your talented employees will see *other* grass as greener. Consider talking with your employees about moves in several directions.

Possible Career Options

- Enrichment: Growing in place

- Lateral movement: Moving across or horizontally

- Exploration: Temporary moves intended for researching other options

- Realignment: Moving downward to open new opportunities

If you notice that three of these options (all but enrichment) raise the possibility of your talented people moving away from you, you're right. If this makes you nervous, you're in the majority. If you've built a strong, functioning team, you don't want to lose key talent to other managers and other parts

GO TO

Career
page 18

of the organization. Some managers are so fearful that they hoard their talent, failing to expose them to other opportunities. Ironically, that strategy backfires and some of the best people walk—often to the competitor.

So why should you help your best people expand their options, even if it means they leave your team? Here are some possibilities:

- People love to work for someone who cares enough to help them with their careers. They'll actually stay a little longer with a development-minded manager.

- Your efforts could save talent for the enterprise. This is truly your job.

- You will gain a reputation as a manager who cares about people and their development. That reputation will draw other talented people your way.

- You may gain personal satisfaction from helping others develop.

Enrichment

GO TO

Enrich
page 37

This is probably the most important option to discuss—but it's also one of the most ignored. Most folks seem to think they need to move out of their current position to develop. Never has this been less true. Most of your employees' work is changing constantly. Job enrichment means a change in what your employees do (content) or how they do it (process), and it inevitably involves learning.

Here's the critical question for you (and them) to ponder: What can employees do, or learn to do, that will energize their work and bring them closer to achieving their goals and the goals of the organization?

> I worked for a great boss as a project manager, but I knew (and she really knew, too) that I could do more. I had fantastic artistic skills (if I do say so myself), and my boss did something about it. She sent me to graphic recording school and has used my new skills in her business. I am thrilled!
>
> —Project manager

Be sure your employees understand that enrichment goals can prepare them for future moves and enhance or add to their skills.

To Do

For clues about potential enrichment opportunities, ask your employees these questions:

★ What do you enjoy most about your job?

★ What could be added to your job to make it more satisfying?

★ What assignment would advance you further in your current work?

★ Which of your current tasks is the most routine? Who might you train to take this over?

Building on the new information, develop a plan with your employees that would help them move toward a meaningful personal goal.

Lateral Movement

Until recently, lateral moves meant that your career might be headed for a dead end. Not today. Lateral moves offer much-needed breadth of experience and are often key to achieving one's career goals.

> *With IBM operating across different segments, the employees who join have the flexibility to move across divisions. So we have had employees who move from IBM Daksh to IBM Research Labs to our Global Technology Services Division. And this happens at mid as well as senior levels. We encourage high performers to move across business units every two to three years, and this prevents stagnation in their careers.[14]*

Taking a lateral move should mean applying current experience in a new job at the same level, but with different duties or challenges. Help employees see that lateral moves can improve skills or shift them from a slow-growing function to an expanding part of the organization.

To Do

To trigger ideas about potential lateral moves, ask your employees questions like these:

★ Which of your skills can be applied beyond your present job and present department?

★ If you make a lateral move, what long-term career opportunities would it provide?

★ What three skills are most transferable to another department?

★ What other department interests you?

Once you're armed with answers to these questions you can begin to explore lateral move opportunities *with* your talented employees.

Exploration

It happens. We reach a stage in our careers when we aren't sure of what we want or what choices are available or even what's appropriate. We need information to decide if the grass is indeed greener elsewhere. Encourage your people to consider options like these:

• Taking short-term job assignments in other parts of the organization or in other parts of the world

• Participating on project teams with people from other departments

• Scheduling informational interviews (These are interviews with people whose job your employee *thinks* he or she wants.)

Giving a talented person whose expertise you need the chance to explore other teams isn't easy. But people are less likely to feel trapped in their current jobs when they have other choices. They may find out that the grass isn't greener.

GO TO
Opportunities
page 138

To Do

For exploration ideas, ask your employees the following questions:

★ What other areas of the company interest you?

★ If you could start your career over, what would you do differently?

★ Which of our current organization task forces interest you? Which might give you the best view of another part of this organization?

★ Whose job would you like to learn more about?

Now, discuss the "so what" of their answers. Who might they talk to next about these possibilities?

Realignment

In the old world of "up is the only way," moving downward would probably be last on anyone's list of options. But sometimes the path to a career goal involves a step back to gain a better position for the next move. Realignment can relieve job stress or allow a graceful return to a role as an individual contributor.

Alas

An excellent technical contributor was promoted to manager. At first he liked the work. It still had some technical components, and he managed other bright individual contributors. But over time he moved more and more into managing those bright others, searching for ways to bring more work to the unit, and fighting administrative battles. He felt he had made a mistake and longed to return to a technical position. He had outgrown his previous position but wanted something with the new hardware group. He went to his manager to admit his mistake and request a move. His manager resisted, suggesting he give it more time or that he enroll in a training course to improve his management skills. Instead, he applied for and got a job that was precisely what he wanted—with a competitor.

This company lost a talented person because neither he nor his manager discussed realignment.

To Do

When considering realignment as an option, ask these questions:

★ If you take an assignment in another area, what will be the new opportunities for growth and development?

★ How could a realigned position enable you to use the skills you really enjoy?

★ Do you miss the technical, hands-on work you used to do?

The answers to these questions can provide a wake-up call for your talented employees. Help them think about the pluses and the minuses of making this move.

When Up Is the Only Way

Sometimes, up is the only choice. Yes, vertical advancement up the corporate ladder is the classic move. Your job is to identify and communicate what a talented employee's vertical options could include. Of course, advancement is most likely when an employee's abilities match the needs of the organization. You must interpret the organization's strategic direction to your team so that they select assignments that will prepare them for coming changes and openings.

Clearly, technical excellence and political savvy are both critical to gaining that next step. Talented people need straight feedback and continual coaching to reach their vertical career goals. As you hold this discussion, remind your employees about two key considerations:

- Always use the current job to ready yourself for vertical moves, and

- Talk with others who are in the desired position to better understand all aspects of the job.

To Do

When discussing possible promotions with your employees, ask them questions like these:

★ Who is your competition for that next position? What are the other person's strengths and weaknesses?

★ How has your job performance been during the last year? How has it prepared you for the next step?

★ What's in it for this company to move you up?

★ What are the satisfactions and headaches that might come with this vertical move?

The More Choices, the Better

Consider . . .	If your employee . . .
Lateral	Wants to gain experience or skills in new areas
	Wants to use skills in a faster growth area or with new people
Enrichment	Wants to accomplish a better job fit
	Wants a change in pace
	Wants to use new skills or put old skills back to work
Vertical	Wants more responsibility and authority
Exploration	Isn't sure what else to do or where else to go
Realignment	Wants to relieve job stress
	Wants to move back to a technical job from management
	Wants to move to a new career path

After reading this chapter, one manager said, "This seems like a lot of asking. Shouldn't my employees come to me with their thoughts and requests about their careers?" Sure they should. But sometimes they won't. They'll be quiet; they'll wait for you to offer up an interesting option—and they'll leave when it doesn't happen. An Asian colleague said, "Employees are generally hesitant to speak out about their career plans because it is perceived as being a 'go-getter' and not loyal to the current boss." Similarly, in Latin America, employees are likely to *wait to be asked* to move into a new role.

Bottom Line

Helping employees reach their goals often means helping them consider moves they may not have seriously considered before. Ask the questions from this chapter to help them see what they could gain by trying a move that isn't a simple vertical step. The more options you can *create with them,* the more you will increase your organization's chances of keeping treasured talent.

Note: One reason talented people leave is because their manager hoarded them. You may have to let them go to let them grow. You might lose them from your team but save them for the enterprise!

EIGHT

Hire

FIT IS IT

*Ponder this: What's your hiring "hit rate?" How many
turn out to be stars who stay and produce at their peak?*

You've heard the adage "start with the end in mind," right? The perfect end-ing is that the people you work so hard to recruit turn out to be exactly right for the jobs you hire them to do! They love being on your team and working for you. And they stay for a while.

The love 'em approach to engaging and retaining talent starts with the hiring process. Why? Because getting the right people in the door in the first place increases the odds of keeping them. As the manager, you have the clearest sense of the "right fit" for your department. Seems logical, doesn't it? Yet some managers see selection as a less important part of their jobs. They spend little time identifying the critical success factors for a position, prepar-ing and conducting excellent interviews based on those factors, and, finally, evaluating and comparing the candidates before making a hiring decision. They may even delegate much of the hiring process to human resources instead of being involved themselves.

Hiring is, in fact, among the most important tasks you have as a manager, and you'll be doing a lot more of it, as Baby Boomers (the largest generation in the workforce) continue to leave the workplace and you search for their replacements. Globally, hiring remains a critical engagement and retention strategy. And it doesn't stop with the job offer. Today re-recruiting your best people is as critical as hiring them in the first place. More about that later.

What Is Right Fit?

How do you know if a candidate will fit? How do you measure fit, manage your biases, and make more objective hiring decisions? Here is a start.

Measuring Fit

When a person has skills and interests that match the job requirements, and core values that are consistent with the organization's values, you have "right fit."

Southwest Airlines looks for fit, especially with the company culture. A pilot told us about his own interview and selection process. He had heard that Southwest managers "hire for attitude and train for skill." The interviews they conducted with him certainly seemed to support that rumor. Through multiple interviews, he realized that the interviewers seemed to care more about who he was as a person than the fact that he had a stellar aviation background that should have made him an obvious choice. They probed for attitudes, beliefs, and behaviors that would give them clues about how he might treat flight attendants or peers, how he might deal with conflict at work, and what mattered most to him.

Southwest managers tested his sense of humor in many ways during the series of interviews, and it became clear to him that they were truly

*looking for a fit between the way work gets done at Southwest Airlines and
his personality.*

Why does Southwest care about an employee's sense of humor, especially
the pilot's? Because Southwest's values include providing "outrageous customer service" and having *fun* at work.

"Fit" also means alignment between the job requirements and the candidate's skills and interests. How often have you seen employees leave (on
their own or with a push) because they simply did not have the right skills
or interests? Why didn't the hiring manager see the problem at the outset?
How can you avoid that expensive mistake? Do your homework, be prepared, and be clear about your wants and needs.

To Do

★ **Analyze the job.** Get input from others to clarify the tasks, traits, and style
required. Then create interview questions that will help you decide if the person has these skills or traits. (See the case study in the next section.)

★ **Create an interview guide with your carefully crafted behavioral questions.**
(Read on for some examples.) Behavioral questions allow you to learn how candidates have handled certain situations. Their answers will help you predict
their ability to handle similar situations in the future. Use the same questions
for all candidates so that you can make fair comparisons.

★ **Include others in the interview process.** Have potential team members and
peers of these future employees interview them (ideally asking different questions from yours) and give you their input. Several heads are definitely better
than one when it comes to hiring.

★ **Consider using personality and skill assessments to help you make the decision.** Get information from your human resources department about tools
that might help you evaluate candidates' skills, work interests, and even values.
Note: Don't rely on just one tool when making your decision.

GO TO

Values
page 217

In Search of Fit

Ramesh, a manager in a high-tech global firm, has an opening for a supervisor in the marketing department in Switzerland. He has placed Internet and newspaper ads and netted a stack of résumés to consider. With help from his human resources representative, he has narrowed the field to the top 10 candidates. On paper, all 10 have technical skills that are great fits for the job.

Ramesh is pretty savvy and has hired many people. Some worked out well, and some were absolute flops. All had looked good on paper. This time, though, Ramesh is prepared to get the right fit! He has identified his department's core *values*. They include honesty, integrity, teamwork, customer focus, and work/life balance.

The critical leadership competencies for the role include motivating others, building a team, and dealing with ambiguity. Ramesh knows that the right fit will be a person with those skills. Next, Ramesh creates his interview guide with the questions he thinks can help him. Here are four questions on his sheet:

1. Tell me about a work incident when you were totally honest, despite a potential risk or downside for the honesty.

2. How did you handle a recent situation where the direction from above was unclear and circumstances were changing?

3. Describe how you motivated a group of people to do something they did not want to do.

4. Tell me about the last global move you made and what was hardest about it.

These questions may seem tough to answer, and they are. You can imagine that each of these questions leads Ramesh and his candidates into potentially deep discussions that could reveal where each candidate truly lines up on the value or leadership competency at hand. The questions are open-ended, so they can't be answered yes or no. They are behavioral, forcing the candidates to cite real-life examples.

Ramesh probes to learn more and takes notes so he will not forget some of their more critical answers or the assumptions he makes along the way. Of course, he asks questions to validate their technical expertise. Afterward, he compares notes with the other interviewers and looks at the assessment results to see if there are any red flags he should explore in follow-up interviews.

Ramesh compares his candidates by scoring them on a 1–5 scale (using 1 to indicate the absence of a skill and 5 to indicate a highly developed skill) on each of the critical success factors that he had identified for the job, including these:

- Technical skills (including language fluency)
- Leadership competencies
- Values

As he scores them, he reviews his notes and thinks about these additional points:

- The level of each candidate's sincerity
- Expressed enthusiasm and interest in the work
- Probable level of skill

While there is no such thing as a totally objective interview or selection process, this method allows Ramesh to make the most objective decision possible. He proceeds to offer the job to the candidate who he feels best meets the criteria.

By the way, had none of the candidates measured up to the criteria Ramesh set, he was willing to start over with a new batch of candidates. He had learned from past mistakes that it is too costly to settle for a mediocre hire.

Avoid Desperation Hiring

Love 'em managers care enough to wait for the right fit. They care about the candidates' and the teams' ultimate success and satisfaction.

Our colleagues in Asia tell us that with economic growth, there is a lot of pressure to "get the warm bodies" into the seats, particularly in China, Singapore, and India. When candidates are few and your needs are immediate, you, too, can fall victim to the dangerous syndrome of *desperation hiring*. When your only interview questions are "When can you start?" or "Can you fog a mirror?" (as in, "Are you breathing?"), you know you're in trouble.

If you're tempted to resort to desperation hiring, remember that today's hiring mistake is tomorrow's headache. You know how hard it is to rid your team of the wrong hire. (Someone recently suggested we write a sequel to *Love 'Em* called *How to Lose Your Losers*. Her point is well taken!)

They Are Choosing, Too

A much sought-after new hire, when explaining how he chose which offer to select, said, "They put me first. They asked, 'What do you want to do?' 'What are your ideas?' and so on."

Be aware that today's tech-savvy, talented candidates are well prepared and have many choices. Imagine that they arrive with a grid in their heads (or on their smartphones) that might look like this one. This grid helps the candidate ask you questions, evaluate the opportunity somewhat objectively, and compare yours with other job opportunities.[15]

My wants/needs (candidate)	Your organization	Your competitor	Another job
Compensation			
Perks			
Team			
Geography			
Training			
Creativity			
Vacation			
Opportunities to Advance			

Be prepared to *sell* your organization or team to candidates by addressing the key issues they raise. Treat candidates more like customers than subordinates. Think carefully about what you and your team can offer, and be ready to give specific examples. Whatever your unique selling proposition, recognize it and leverage it during the interview.

Beware: don't oversell. Often an employee's exit is due to unrealistic expectations of the job and organization. If the recruitment process is honest and open, you can avoid the quick exit.

I've left a few companies after being there only three months. In a couple of cases, the projects turned out much less interesting or challenging than management had described. In one particularly bad case, I was told about a system that would have been really interesting, but once I got there and actually started talking with them about the details, I found out that the things they described to me weren't possible technically. The system actually was just a data entry website.

Another time, as a contractor, I was brought in to do software development. Instead, they put me on production support. When my contract was up three months later, I chose, to their dismay, not to continue the contract.

Now I don't trust what they tell me about the position, but other than ask a lot of questions, I can't really do much.

—Software engineer

To Do

★ Remember to sell talented prospects honestly. Think about what makes your company unique and a great place to work.

★ Listen carefully to what candidates are seeking. Be open to possibilities. Example: One company enticed its top choice by changing the job title from *Feed Salesman* to *Livestock Produce Specialist*.

★ Place a copy of this book on your desk during the interview. (Candidates will get the hint that keeping good people is important to you.) To go a step further, show them the book and ask them which of the chapters (A–Z) are most relevant to retaining *them*.

What Do You Assume?

What if "right fit" means *like me* or *the right age* or *shape/size* or *gender* or *color?* It doesn't—or shouldn't. The "right fit" excuse has been used many times to put clones (usually clones of the boss) in jobs. That is certainly not what we mean by "right fit." In fact, if you spend the time to identify those critical factors that spell success for a particular job and then select people using those criteria, you are most apt to avoid dismissing potentially wonderful candidates.

We all have "leanings," and we often make assumptions based on them. Let's test some of your assumptions about getting the right person in the job. Ask yourself, as you read this list, "Have I ever thought this about a person or a job?" Be brutally honest—you don't have to tell anyone how you responded!

GO TO

Dignity
page 27

Assumption Testing

Assumption: Single mothers will be a risk because when their children are ill, they will not show up.

Fact: Some single moms so need this job that they will find a way to make it to work. Some have excellent contingency planning skills and have two or three backup plans when the kids are sick. In fact, the Center for Creative Leadership has reported that being a committed parent can enhance managerial ability, according to a study conducted with Clark University.[16] (And remember—it is illegal to ask candidates if they are single parents or have children.)

Assumption: A seriously overweight person can't do this job because of the air travel required.

Fact: Overweight or obese individuals certainly can find ways of doing the job, even if it demands air travel. Obesity is viewed by law as a disability and, therefore, is protected by the ADA (Americans with Disabilities Act). That means that you must consider accommodation for a candidate who is qualified to do the work.

Assumption: He is too old or too young for this job.

Fact: What's age got to do with it? Architect Frank Lloyd Wright and heart surgeon Michael DeBakey are examples of people who excelled in their crafts after the age of 90.

Assumption: We need a man in this job because it is too challenging for a woman.

Fact: The ability to function well is made up of a combination of traits, skills, behaviors, and experience that is *gender-neutral* (meaning gender does not predict ability).

Assumption: Someone of _____ descent just wouldn't be comfortable or really fit in here.

Fact: If you've ever studied or worked in a multicultural environment you know that a person's heritage has no bearing on his comfort or fit within a particular environment. Think about your own experiences and where you've fit in just fine, despite dramatic language or cultural differences.

When you find yourself forming assumptions about candidates based on their gender, size, accent, attire, or color (and, by the way, we all do that sometimes), then gently move yourself back to the key criteria you have identified and your methodology for assessing all of your candidates fairly.

Note: You can learn a lot about yourself, your organization, and hiring if you have the chance to do some global recruiting. Here's what one recruiter experienced and learned. Thanks to Jeremy Eskinazi of Riviera Advisors.

I was shocked by the appearance of a Confucian candidate who came to interview for a key position in our Asian headquarters. The candidate had a large mole on his face, with a long hair growing out of it. He also had two long pinky fingernails. I'd frankly never seen anything like it and wondered what it was all about. Why wouldn't he have plucked the hair and trimmed the nails? I asked my global partner, who said, "To have a mole brings you very good luck. To have a hair growing out of the mole is even luckier. And it's common for men to grow their pinky nails long to show they are not laborers." As my understanding grew, my impression of this candidate changed for the better.

Now there's some assumption testing for you!

Prevent Quick Quits

Your risk of losing talent is highest in the first three to six months on the job. Why might that be? Too often we choose the right people but fail to support them as they assume their new roles. It is crucial that you extend the handshake in ways that matter to each new hire.

Orientation (also known as onboarding) *and ongoing support* are key pieces of the selection process and will increase the odds of your new hires' success, contribution to and tenure on the team. New hires come to an organization fully charged, excited about their new adventure, and filled with energy and potential. By effectively tapping into that energy, knowledge, and wisdom right from the start, you can maximize the new employee's potential and productivity well past the first year.

We know that many quick quits *can* be prevented. There is a direct correlation between shortened tenure and actions you do, or do not, take (yup, sorry—*you* again). Develop a relationship. Show you care. Start by having conversations with your new employees.

Talk About Relationships

Help them build relationships, and they're more likely to stay. Fill their "lunch cards" for at least the first two weeks. In your early, ongoing conversations, you might ask questions like these:

- What kind of support or direction do you need from me that you aren't getting? What are you getting that you don't want?

- How are you getting along with your other team members? What introductions would you like me to make? Are you finding people to go to lunch with? Are you finding people to go to when you need help?

Talk About the Job

They joined your organization because you offered work they love to do. Are they doing it? If the job doesn't measure up to what you promised, find ways to close the gap. Check in early and often—daily in the beginning. These questions should help:

- How does the job measure up to what we promised so far? Where are we on or off? How might we course-correct?

- What other interests would you like to explore, either now or over time?

Talk About the Organization

The people you carefully recruited and selected are now onboard. Are they wondering who or what they've joined? Early on, ask questions like these:

- How does the work pace and schedule work for you? Is there anything we need to adjust?

- How is our organization the same or different from your last employer? What do you miss most? Least?

- How can I help you get more of what you want from this workplace? We want you to be happy here!

Yes, all this conversation and connecting requires time and energy on your part. But it might just prevent a quick quit!

To Do

★ Meet with your new hires often: daily for the first week, weekly for the first month, once every two weeks for the first quarter, and then at least once a month for the rest of the first year. Build your relationship consistently.

★ Have an "expectations exchange" with your new (and existing) employees. Clearly define what you expect from them and ask what they are expecting from you. Help them understand how their work connects to the corporate strategies.

★ Introduce them to others on your team even before their first day. People with several options could be tempted by another offer before they show up for the first day of work.

★ Spend time teaching them about the organization they have just joined. Tell stories, sharing your experiences and knowledge about the culture and history.

★ Involve your key people in the new hires' orientation. Expose new employees to others' views as well as your own.

★ Mentor and find mentors for them as they work to close the inevitable skill gaps.

★ Observe them—what do they enjoy the most? What's easiest or hardest for them to learn?

★ Develop a learning plan to ensure they are challenged.

★ Ask great questions . . . ongoingly!

Be available to support new hires in this uncertain early stage of their employment. That may mean seeking them out to see how they are doing and conveying that you are behind them all the way.

Marta showed up for her first day of work and found bagels and cream cheese on her desk—lots of them! Then people started coming to introduce themselves, welcome her to the team and get their bagels. Marta's boss said it's one great way to ensure his newly hired talent met everyone on the team—before 10 a.m.

Get creative as you think about ways to welcome *your* new talent!

Re-recruit as Well

But what about the rest of your talent? While you are busy hiring the best-fit candidates for key roles on your team, do a little re-recruiting along the way. Often candidates and new employees are viewed as close to perfect (their warts haven't surfaced yet), and they get all the attention. If you have done a great job of selecting, you will have a whole new collection of stars. Your long-term employees can feel less noticed, less appreciated, and perhaps even taken for granted as you carefully select, orient, and train these new folks. Avoid that dangerous phenomenon by re-recruiting *all* of your talent. Show your current employees that they are important and critical to you and to the success of your team, especially as you recruit new team members.

If you're not recruiting your best people, you're the only one who isn't.

Bottom Line

Great managers are great recruiters. The best never take down their "Help Wanted" sign. *Fit is it* when it comes to hiring. If you get the right people in the right roles in your organization and on your team, you absolutely will increase the odds of retaining them. And don't ever stop re-recruiting your key talent. Remember, your competitors want the talent you've worked so hard to hire.

NINE

Information

SHARE IT

Ponder this: Do you have information?
Do you share it?

In the information age, powerful new businesses exist solely for the purpose of leading you to the information you want. That reality has changed people's attitudes toward having, sharing or hoarding information.

> *The Web will change relationships with employees. We will never again have discussions where knowledge is hidden in somebody's pocket. You will have to lead with ideas, not by controlling information.*
>
> —Jack Welch, former CEO, General Electric

Jack Welch's prediction has come true.

★ ★ ★ ★ ★

What if you don't share information?

> **First:** It's hard for you to do your best without good information. The same is true for your employees.

> **Second:** You will lose your talent—maybe not today, but eventually those with choices will leave you, either physically or psychologically.

Having the Scoop or Being Out of the Loop

As kids, we knew that having the inside scoop is cool, and we felt important if we had information that others did not have. If information is power, then being out of the loop—lacking information—might leave one powerless. People want a boss with influence and power in the organization. Think about your own work experience, and you will probably agree that you would much rather work for someone who is in the loop than for a boss who is clueless. Your employees are no different. They want you to be in the loop.

They want and need you to bring them in the loop too. Your talented people feel they count when you share information with them.

In the Absence of Information, They Will Make It Up

Information sharing during dramatic change is even more critical than during stable times. We have seen dozens of examples of high-level managers deciding to withhold information in organizations going through major change (downsizing, mergers, acquisitions). We've seen middle managers hoarding information out of fear of losing their power or importance. We acknowledge that at times you simply cannot share, but check out what might happen when you withhold information about change:

Senior Manager Thinks	Employees Think
It's too early to tell them.	Silence must mean it's pretty bad.
This news is too frightening—we'd better wait.	They're moving the company to Panama.
I'm afraid if we tell them, productivity will drop.	The company's going belly-up. Where else can I get a job?

Notice that the manager is trying to protect the employees and prevent all the chatter that can put a huge dent in productivity. Ironically, the silence and protection backfire. Productivity plummets as these employees worry about their jobs and update their résumés.

In contrast, where top leaders give information as early and honestly as possible and hold managers accountable for passing the news down, employees actually feel important and valued, minimizing the productivity dip.

Another good reason to share information is that your employees might be able to help. A major hospital offers a good example:

The hospital had a policy of never eliminating positions through layoffs—a commitment it had kept throughout its history, including its merger with another hospital. Several years ago, the policy was tested when the hospital faced a potential $20 million deficit. Management shared the news with the staff and asked for their help. Within 10 days, they received 4,000 cost-saving ideas from employees. Sixteen task forces formed to deal with the ideas. While most of the strategies involved tighter controls on purchasing, employees also suggested forgoing raises and holding off on accrued paid time off. By the end of the year, the task forces had realized enough savings to eliminate the need for layoffs.

Giving Your Fair Share

Love 'em managers share more! They share openly, honestly and often. What about you? How do you know what and how much to share?

To some degree it depends on your organization's culture and management philosophy. At one end of the openness continuum lies the philosophy of Jack Stack, founder of Springfield Remanufacturing Company (SRC) in Springfield, Missouri. He wrote *The Great Game of Business* and *A Stake in the Outcome,* and he espouses "open book management," a set of beliefs and business practices that dozens of highly successful organizations have adopted. He says, "We are building a company in which everyone tells the truth every day—not because everyone is honest, but because everyone has access to the same information: operating metrics, financial data, valuation estimates. The more people understand what's really going on in their company, the more eager they are to help solve its problems."[17] It's clear that when Jack Stack says "open book," he means tell it all!

On the other end of the continuum lie more secretive, sometimes even strongly paternalistic cultures. A participant in a training program in Asia told us that in his organization, managers are more like parents, who need to protect and care for their children. They might tell overly positive stories about the company and downplay threats and upcoming changes—all in the attempt to shield people from the news.

Consider the consequences of your communication style and the culture in which you manage. Do what you can to share information with your employees. You'll increase commitment and enhance the odds of keeping your best people.

GO TO

Career
page 18

No, You Don't Need a Crystal Ball

Your team expects you to help them look to the future. That includes providing information that supports your employees' development. You need to share what you know about

- your organization's strategic direction and goals;

- your profession, industry, and organization's future;

- the emerging trends and new developments that may affect career possibilities; and

- the cultural and political realities of your organization.

As you forecast, your team members will learn to look broadly at their profession, industry, and organization and see the trends and implications. They will also feel more competent and confident in their future marketability.

To Do

★ Forward articles about your industry for your employees to read. You might have access to industry-based blogs, newsletters, reports, and magazines that they aren't aware of. Share critical information that can help them make decisions about their career development.

★ State the organization's business strategies and vision—again. If you think that's a waste of your valuable time, think again.

★ Ask your talented people what information they want from you, when they want it, and in what form they'd like to get it.

Inquiring Minds

Have you ever had a boss tell you, "I knew that weeks ago but couldn't [or decided not to] share it with you"? Isn't that infuriating? You may have thought, "Thanks a lot. A lot of good this does me now!" or "See if I trust you in the future," or "Why even tell me you knew? Is this a power trip?"

A CEO accepted the resignation of a member of his senior team and knew there would be an impact on the organization. When we asked him when he planned to share that information with his key players, he responded, "I don't want to upset them during a tense time, so I think I'll wait until our staff meeting in two days."

What do you think? Good idea? No, bad idea. What are the odds that people wouldn't find out about the resignation the same day? People knew within the hour and were frustrated, disappointed, and even angry that the CEO had not informed them immediately. Many felt distrusted, even undervalued by their boss as a result of his nondisclosure.

Alas

We were working on a large government-sponsored program and spent hours preparing for a major "proof of concept" demonstration. In the meantime, our boss was in higher-level discussions with the client, in which the client shared the fact that the entire program was going through a big funding review and that the plug might be pulled before the demonstration took place. We didn't hear about it until the day of the demonstration. Then we learned how close we had come to the demonstration never taking place. We felt disenfranchised and undervalued. Had he shared the seriousness of the situation with us, we could have produced other supporting arguments and generated other scenarios that would have helped our client to support the program with his superiors.

Our boss probably thought he was shielding us from things we didn't need to worry about, or he thought we wouldn't give 100 percent if we knew about this conversation. He didn't place much value on our ability to contribute; it felt paternalistic and elitist. After that, my trust level with my manager was never the same. I think the whole team felt the same way.

—Senior engineer, large engineering research institute

So, as a manager, when should you share information? *The sooner the better!* When you are clear about what you want or need to share, find a way to do it soon, especially if the information is about a major change. Here are some *trigger events* that might alert you to the need for information giving:

- Merger or acquisition

- Online or print article about the company

- A requisition for a key position

- New hires

- An overactive rumor mill

How to Share

Remember that the primary focus of this book is how to keep your talented employees. Volumes have been written about communication strategies, in both normal times and during times of dramatic change. Face-to-face communication, social media, video, newsletter, blogs, e-mail, voice mail, all-hands meetings, and bulletin boards all have their place in communicating effectively. Our question is: Which approach works best, given your organization's culture and the message you are trying to send?

Here are some guidelines:

To Do

★ Share information face-to-face, especially if it is difficult to deliver or will affect your employees significantly. Tell your direct reports the news yourself, rather than having them learn it via e-mail or from some other source. Let your supervisors give the news to their direct reports also. Research shows that people believe it and react more favorably when the news comes from their direct supervisor. If it has to travel through several layers, double-check to be sure the message is getting through.

★ Get creative. The more creatively you send a message, the greater the chance your employees will notice it. Consider doing the unexpected. If people are used to hearing news via e-mail, try face-to-face or video next time.

Close to the Vest?

Building an information-rich culture can be challenging. After all, there will be times when you have information that you simply cannot share. A few simple guidelines can help you handle the situation appropriately without alienating your employees. When you must hold information in confidence, keep these tips in mind:

- Never use information withholding as a power tool. If you receive proprietary or "secret" information, do not tell people you have it unless they ask you.

- If people ask you if you have information, be honest. Tell them that you are not at liberty to share, and tell them why. For example, you could say, "The information is sensitive or proprietary," or "I have been asked to keep it confidential, and I need to honor that request."

- Be prepared for the possibility that your responses may not please people. If you establish a track record of early, honest information sharing, you will have more room to withhold information when you must.

It's a Two-Way Street

Getting information is also a way of keeping your employees. Your job is to share it *and* to seek it! People want to be heard regarding their jobs, the work at hand, and the organization's goals and strategies. As a manager, you need to ask for that input.

> *When I started visiting the plants and meeting with employees, what was reassuring was the tremendous, positive energy in our conversations. One man said he had been with the company for 25 years and hated every minute of it—until he was asked for his opinion. He said that question transformed his job.*
>
> *—VP in a global pharmaceutical company*

While most managers expect employees to come to them if there is a problem, often employees don't feel comfortable or managers don't offer the opportunity. Help your employees feel comfortable talking to you by scheduling regular opportunities for those talks.

Too Much of a Good Thing?

Do you ever feel like there's just too much information coming your way? One survey of 1,700 white-collar workers in five countries (United States, China, South Africa, the United Kingdom, and Australia) found professionals in every market struggling to cope and asking their employers for ways to deal with information overload.[18]

The information avalanche causes some workers to say they're reaching a breaking point and that they feel demoralized when they can't manage all the information that comes their way at work. What can you do to relieve that stress? Ask your employees if they're getting enough or too much information from you or from their colleagues. Brainstorm solutions with the teams you manage. Establish agreements with them about how to increase effectiveness by decreasing the quantity and increasing the quality of information flowing their way.

Bottom Line

Information is a form of currency on the job. How you spend it and how you acquire it has a big impact on your ability to engage and retain talented people. Stay in the loop. Keep your employees in the loop. It will help you keep your talent.

TEN

Jerk
DON'T BE ONE

Ponder this: Are you one? Occasionally?

—WARNING—

If this book landed on your desk
with a bookmark here, pay attention!

We've all worked with or for people who exhibit "jerklike" behaviors. You know, they're the ones that shout, humiliate, fail to listen, demand perfection, show disrespect, betray trust, simply don't care—and the list goes on.

And if the word *jerk* doesn't exactly translate for you, how about one of these words?

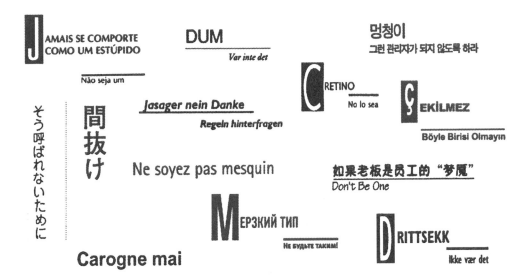

In Greek, we hear that there are at least 20 words that mean "jerk."

No matter what the name for it, people in every culture and in every company occasionally, sometimes accidentally, exhibit jerklike behaviors. A recent study found that in India 56 percent of employees report being bullied by their boss.[19] Another study found that three out of four employees report that their boss is the worst and most stressful part of their job and that 65 percent of employees say they'd take a new boss over a pay raise.[20]

People cautioned us not to write this chapter or at least not to use this title. But to avoid this topic is to avoid discussing a primary reason why people leave their jobs. If employees don't like their bosses, they will leave even when they are well paid, receive recognition, and have a chance to learn and grow. In fact, disliking the boss is one of the top causes of talent loss. Take a look at this exit interview:

Interviewer: *Gerardo, why have you decided to leave the organization? I know that we pay competitively and you just received a bonus.*

Gerardo: *Is this confidential?*

Interviewer: *Definitely, yes.*

Gerardo: *The pay is fine. The work is fine. But my boss is impossible. He is so difficult to work with, and I've decided life is too short to spend it working for a jerk.*

Have you ever worked for a jerk? Are there any jerks in your organization?

We've received dozens of "jerk" stories from our readers. Here are some of the toppers.

Alas After Alas

"My boss told me I was passed over for promotion because I hadn't gotten over my grief soon enough following my father's death."

"My boss told me to come talk to him anytime. I went in for a topic important to me: my career. He kept reading (even answering) his e-mail while I talked. Guess how important I felt."

"My first job out of college, my boss wanted me to cancel my vacation when the client requested deadline changes. However, he wouldn't cancel his trip to Greece!"

"The boss I refer to as 'Mr. Toxic' told me in a memo that I was getting too fat to represent the company professionally."

"I had a boss who would drop his pencil on my side of the desk when I was pregnant. He thought it was funny to watch me struggle to pick it up."

"Prior to a meeting my boss said, 'You take charge, run the meeting, assert your authority.' During the meeting, the boss continually interrupted, contradicted, and undermined my authority, even though I followed our pre-set agenda."

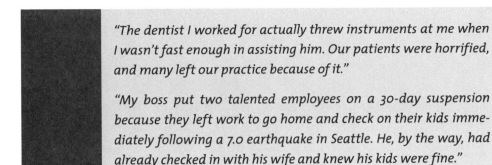

"The dentist I worked for actually threw instruments at me when I wasn't fast enough in assisting him. Our patients were horrified, and many left our practice because of it."

"My boss put two talented employees on a 30-day suspension because they left work to go home and check on their kids immediately following a 7.0 earthquake in Seattle. He, by the way, had already checked in with his wife and knew his kids were fine."

"A boss in China made headlines when he assigned the homework of his 12-year-old daughter to his employees. It wasn't the first time and the employees stayed up late two nights in a row completing the task and dealing with the demanding girl."

Hard to believe? Maybe not. Unfortunately, most of us have worked for a jerk at some point in our lives. Most of us escaped!

This chapter is not about labeling people as jerks and letting the rest of us off the hook. It is about defining jerklike behaviors and the "jerk mode" that people occasionally assume. It is about learning to assess whether you exhibit those behaviors and how often. And it's about trying to change for the better. Why? To engage, motivate, and keep your talented people.

What Is a Jerk?

We asked dozens of people, "What do jerks act like or look like?" (The book and movie *The Devil Wears Prada* certainly portrayed some of the worst of these behaviors, but our research found many more.) This checklist reflects what we heard.[21] We dare you to score yourself.

Behavior Checklist

Instructions: Score yourself on the following behaviors, using a 0–5 scale: 0 means you never act this way, and 5 means you often act this way.

How often do you:	0–5
Intimidate	_____
Condescend or demean	_____
Act arrogant	_____
Withhold praise	_____
Slam doors, pound tables	_____
Swear	_____
Behave rudely	_____
Belittle people in front of others	_____
Micromanage	_____
Manage up, not down	_____
Always look out for number one	_____
Give mostly negative feedback	_____
Yell at people	_____
Tell lies or "half-truths"	_____
Act above the rules	_____
Enjoy making people sweat	_____
Act superior to or smarter than everyone else	_____
Show disrespect	_____
Act sexist	_____
Act bigoted	_____
Withhold critical information	_____
Use inappropriate humor	_____
Blow up in meetings	_____
Start every sentence with "I"	_____
Steal credit or the spotlight from others	_____
Block career moves (prevent promotion or hold onto "stars")	_____

Distrust most people   _____

Show favoritism   _____

Humiliate and embarrass others   _____

Criticize often (at a personal level)   _____

Overuse sarcasm   _____

Deliberately ignore or isolate some people   _____

Set impossible goals or deadlines   _____

Never accept blame, let others take the hit   _____

Undermine authority   _____

Show lack of caring for people   _____

Betray trust or confidences   _____

Gossip/spread rumors   _____

Act as if others are stupid   _____

Have "sloppy moods" (when feeling down, take it out on others)   _____

Use fear as a motivator   _____

Show revenge   _____

Interrupt constantly   _____

Make "bad taste" remarks   _____

Fail to listen   _____

Lack patience   _____

Demand perfection   _____

Break promises   _____

Second-guess constantly   _____

Have to always be in control   _____

Total score: _____

Note: This is an insight tool, meant to help you evaluate which of these behaviors you might occasionally, accidentally exhibit. To learn more, check out our Jerk Survey on www.keepem.com. The following interpretation guidelines are just that—guidelines.

Interpretation Guidelines

0–20   Although you have a bad day now and then, you are probably not viewed as a jerk. Watch those behaviors for which you scored above a 3, and get more feedback from your employees.

21–60   Look out! You could be viewed as a jerk by some, at least in some situations. Commit to identifying and working on your jerklike behaviors.

61 or more   You are at high risk for losing talent. Get more feedback and get some help (maybe a coach).

If you checked none of the behaviors on this assessment, you might be a saint. (Take it home to your family and friends and test again!) In other words, most of us do exhibit some of these behaviors some of the time. The question is, how many and how often? And what effect does your behavior have on the people who report to you? Often, leaders are the last to know that their style is off-putting. Watch for drops in productivity, difficulty hiring, lateral moves out of your department, and, of course, turnover.

Warren Bennis gave his view of a firing for dishonesty at the New York Times. *"It doesn't matter how many prizes you win if you damage your real prize—your talent—in the process. Uncaring, arrogant leadership that values accolades at any cost is always inappropriate, but especially ill-suited to idea-driven organizations such as the* Times. *Whatever their titles or official positions, talented people have their own power. They have the power to walk. They will not stay in an organization that treats them like cattle, even if the name on the building is as august as the* New York Times. *Raines and his more imperious predecessors polarized their staffs and made them compete with each other for newsroom resources, including the favor of the executive editor. Such intramural competition ends up making people less creative, not more creative."*

Bennis pointed out that part of the problem was the leadership of the executive editor, Howell Raines. "Raines was an ego-driven autocrat who ruled by fear, played favorites, had an idiosyncratic news judgment, and loathed hearing unwanted truths."[22]

Consider the Cost

A *McKinsey Quarterly* article featured a company that calculated the extra cost (or TCJ = total cost of jerks) that one star salesperson generated—the assistants he burned through, the overtime costs, the legal costs, the anger management training, and so on. The extra cost of one jerk for one year was $160,000.[23]

Another study found that stress and lost productivity related to incivility cost the U.S. economy multibillion dollars annually. There's even a book written on the topic: *The Cost of Bad Behavior: How Incivility Is Damaging Your Business and What to Do About It,* by Christine Porath (2009).

Jerklike behavior ends up costing more than just dollars. From headaches to heart attacks, the stress of working for a jerk takes a physical toll. And what about the emotional, psychological side of this equation? Could you be ruining your employee's marriage? It may sound extreme, but think about the last time you felt beat up at work and headed home to spill the nastiness all over your family. You get the picture.

To Do

Check out this list, courtesy of Robert Sutton, author of *The No Asshole Rule*.[24] Which of these effects of jerklike behavior do you see in your organization? Which have you experienced yourself?

★ Distraction from tasks because of efforts to avoid encounters with the "jerk boss"

★ Loss of motivation on the job

★ Physical illness because of stress

★ Frequent absenteeism

★ Reduction in innovation

★ Inability to attract top talent

★ Increased disengagement

Who, Me?

We spend a lot of time teaching leaders what to do. We don't spend enough time teaching leaders what to stop. Half the leaders I have met don't need to learn what to do. They need to learn what to stop.

—Management expert Peter Drucker, as quoted by Marshall Goldsmith in What Got You Here Won't Get You There *(2007)*

Give your results from the jerk checklist some serious thought. Ask your friends at work to look at the list with you and give you honest feedback. (If you don't have any friends, that may be a clue.) Ask family members to give you insight as well. If others agree that you *often* exhibit more than one or two of those behaviors, you are at high risk for losing talent.

Jerklike behaviors are so damaging that even one or two can negate all of your other strengths as a boss.

I had no idea that my employees viewed me as such a jerk. We had 360-degree feedback (input from boss, peers, subordinates, even customers) as a part of a leadership development program. Employees had a chance to type in comments at the end of a lengthy computerized survey. My employees basically told me that I came across as insensitive and uncaring. They said that my drive to get results seemed to be at any cost, including employee health and morale. I was so shocked at this feedback. I felt terrible. Now I'm working

with a coach to help me figure out how to change my behaviors. The first step
was finding out how my employees viewed me.

—Senior manager, engineering firm

If you have never had an in-depth 360-degree feedback assessment, consider it. The feedback should come to you anonymously, and you should use it for your own awareness and development. Recognizing your ineffective and potentially damaging behaviors is the first step to doing something about them.

GO TO

Truth
page 196

Once a Jerk, Always a Jerk?

Just as you can learn new leadership skills at any age, you can stop ineffective behaviors or replace them with more effective ones.

I used to blow up at people. When I was under stress, and someone said the
wrong thing, I just lost control. I yelled, turned red in the face, and pounded
the table. The result was that people used to tiptoe around me. They hid bad
news and took few risks, fearing my temper if they failed. People were intimi-
dated. We lost creativity, productivity, and some talent along the way—all
because of my uncontrolled temper.

Now I'm better, at least 90 percent of the time. It took some time and a
lot of effort, but I now have a handle on my emotions. When I feel the blood
pressure rise and my anger coming on, I picture a stop sign. I stop, take three
slow, deep breaths, and then we talk about the problem. What a difference—
both in how I feel about myself and how my employees react.

—Manager, marketing and sales department

Because behaviors are learned, we know that it is possible to change. It may not be easy, but it is possible. The difficulty of changing ineffective behaviors depends on the answers to several questions:

- How ingrained is the behavior? Have you been acting this way for 50 years or for 3? Some of those long-term habits are certainly more difficult to break than those you learned more recently.

- Are you crystal-clear about what the desired behavior will look like? A clear picture of the goal will certainly make it easier to get there.

- Do you have resources available to help you? It's easier to change if you have people supporting you.

- How complex is the behavior? You may be able to decide simply to stop telling off-color jokes and never do it again. Negative reactions under stress are more complicated and interwoven, so they will probably require more focus, more resources, and a longer time to change. You may need to develop a new repertoire of behaviors.

- Do you really want to change? Why? If you can't answer this question, you will not change. You've got to want to.

Once you decide to change, you can create your action plan.

When he was CEO of PepsiCo, Andy Pearson was named one of the toughest bosses in America, based on his ability to inflict pain and humiliation. He brought talented people to tears with his words and proved he was smart by finding fault with other people's ideas. He was heard saying to key employees, "A room full of monkeys could do better than this!" Pearson realized late in life that he could be more effective if he led differently. He now seeks answers and ideas from employees at all levels, rather than issuing orders. He believes his job is to listen to the people who work for him and to serve them.[25]

To Do

★ Get honest feedback somehow. You need a clear picture of how you look to others.

★ Ask, "So what?" Think about the implications of your behaviors. Are they getting in the way of your effectiveness? Are they causing good people to leave?

★ Take a stress management course.

★ Exercise. Eat well. Sleep more. You choose.

★ Try tai chi, yoga, meditation, or prayer.

★ If you decide to change, seek help from others:

- Get a coach.

- Seek counseling.

- Attend a personal growth seminar.

- Read self-improvement books.

- Ask people to monitor and give you feedback as you attempt to change.

★ Be patient with yourself and with others. It takes time to change behaviors. And it takes time for others to trust you—especially if you've exhibited jerklike behaviors for a long time!

Bottom Line

If you believe (or find out) that you often exhibit jerklike behaviors, decide to change. This entire book exists to help you do it. Changing jerklike behaviors may be the most important action you can take to keep your talent on your team.

ELEVEN

GET SOME

Ponder this: Do you hold the "all work, no play" philosophy—where work is simply not the place for fun?

How do you feel about fun at work? Do you believe in it? Have it? Support it? Make it happen? Discourage it? Evaluate your own assumptions about fun at work. Then consider creating and supporting kicks in the workplace as one way to keep your best people.

Research shows that a fun-filled workplace generates enthusiasm—and that enthusiasm leads to increased productivity, better customer service, a positive attitude about the company, and higher odds that your talent will stay.

Fun for One—Fun for All?

When was the last time you had fun at work?

- Last year?

- Last month?

- Last week?

- Yesterday?

If your answer was yesterday, you're probably smiling as you read this.

★ ★ ★ ★ ★

Of course, one person's fun can be another person's turnoff.

> *Management, Regarding Personal Days at Work—Each employee will receive 104 personal days a year. They are called Saturdays and Sundays.*

Did you grin? Grimace? Groan—especially in today's 24/7 work world? Telling jokes may be fun for you and ridiculous (or even insulting) to someone else. Some people get kicks out of decorating your office as a birthday surprise, while others love to take a break to debate some current hot topic or to surf the Web. So remember to ask people, "What makes work more fun?"

GO TO
Ask
page 1

> *Humorize, and you humanize the workplace.*
>
> —Fran Solomon, senior vice empress, Playfair, Inc.

Fun-Free Zone

Unfortunately, many workplaces are fun-free zones. If your employees were to grade you on the degree to which you support fun at work, what would you get? If you say, "I'd get a C+," why is that? Maybe you just were not raised that way. The bosses you learned from may have been fun-averse, serious taskmasters. Perhaps you believe that allowing fun at work will cause you to lose control or fail to achieve results. You might think that moments of levity will set bad precedents, and the group will never get back to business. Some of your concerns may be based on *fun myths* about having kicks in the workplace.

To Do

Check which of these myths you tend to believe in:

★ Myth 1: Professionalism and fun are incompatible.

★ Myth 2: It takes toys and money to have fun.

★ Myth 3: Fun means laughter.

★ Myth 4: You have to plan for fun.

★ Myth 5: Fun time at work will compromise our results.

★ Myth 6: You have to have a good sense of humor (or be funny) to create a fun work environment.

Myth Debunking

These myths are just that—myths. Let's debunk them.

Myth 1: Professionalism and Fun Are Incompatible.

Can you have fun and still maintain a professional work environment? It depends on the kind of fun you are talking about. Slapstick silliness (pie-in-the-face humor) will not fit well in a business-suit environment. But there are many appropriate ways to get some kicks in even the most buttoned-up workplace.

Every month we had client reports due and most of us dreaded the solitary extra-hours work that the task required. So we started planning to stay late one night each month. We went to a deli for snacks and good wine and then held a work party. We were all on our own computers in our own offices, but we took regular breaks, helped each other, enjoyed our food and wine together, and had some laughs in the after-work casual environment. It not only made the monthly task much more enjoyable, but it provided a type of team building.

—Consultant, management consulting firm

In another highly professional work environment, when someone is late to a meeting, they either have to sing a song or tell a new joke (in good taste!). People are on time more often since the new rule, but there is also a guaranteed chuckle as people slide in the door a minute or two late.

Most concern about having fun in a serious workplace is actually concern about inappropriate humor, loud behavior, or poor timing. If employees' timing is off or their behavior is embarrassing or disruptive, give them that feedback, just as you would about any work behaviors. Having fun at work might actually be an acquired skill for some people. You can help them get better at it!

Myth 2: It Takes Toys and Money to Have Fun at Work.

This is the sister myth to "It takes toys and money to have fun in life." When we asked dozens of people to reflect on fun times they remembered having at work, here is what we heard. (Notice how many of these examples cost money or involve toys.)

- "No specific time. It was just the day-to-day laughter my colleagues and I shared—mostly about small things."

- "We decorated my boss's office for his birthday. We used five bags of confetti from the shredding machine."

- "Spontaneous after-work trips to the local pizza parlor."

- "Verbal sparring with my brainy, funny colleagues."

- "When we had a huge project, a tight deadline, and we had to work all night. I wouldn't want to do that often, but we had a good time, laughs in the middle of the night, and a thrill when we finished the project."

- "Receiving this poem from my dedicated, funny employees whom I sent to Detroit on business: 'Roses are red, violets are blue, it's 30 below, and we hate you.'"

- "In the midst of a big stressful project, our boss took us to a local park for a volleyball game during lunch. We still talk about it."

Toys and money certainly can help you have fun, too. Employees in a Danish company use water pistols to discourage mistimed critical thinking during creative brainstorming events.

Microsoft and Amgen are two global companies with "fun" budgets. In both companies, people are expected to work hard and play hard. Their play includes the occasional extravagant party or boat trip. Although employees greatly appreciate elaborate outings, most report that it is the day-to-day work environment that matters most. It has to be enjoyable.

Myth 3: Fun Means Laughter.

Fun often does involve laughter or smiles. Sometimes people just need to take themselves less seriously. Laughter has been called *internal jogging,* as it has the same positive health benefit as an aerobic run. Supposedly this works through the release of endorphins, the healing elements of the body. And, even better, you can lose four pounds of fat a year by laughing an additional 15 minutes a day!

Did you know: Kids laugh, on average, 400 times/day—adults 12. Hang out with a seven-year-old for a day and count!

But people can have fun at work without laughing or getting silly.

In my company we are more formal and serious. You might call our form of kicks, serious fun. We enjoy celebration and togetherness at the end of a project, during Chinese New Year, on family days, or during team exercise or department meals out.

—Colleague in Singapore

An intriguing project and collaboration with wonderful teammates can truly be fun. Work that is meaningful and makes a difference can be fun. Building something new can be fun.

Some of the most fun I ever had was in the early days of creating a completely new form of airplane. We were building something new that would make a difference. It was difficult and challenging but so much fun.

—Retired aeronautical engineer

Myth 4: You Have to Plan for Fun.

Planned fun makes sense sometimes. The employee softball team provides fun and requires planning, as does an occasional employee picnic or the annual holiday party. But a lot of fun in the workplace is spontaneous.

We had been working so hard and had nailed all of our goals for the quarter. My boss called us into his office and presented the team with movie tickets—for the two o'clock show, that day! It was great. We took off as a group and felt like kids, playing hooky from school. It was so spontaneous and so appreciated.

—City government employee

Unplanned fun can be as simple as showing up at the staff meeting with muffins for everyone, asking a group of employees to join you for lunch at a new restaurant, or taking an unplanned coffee break to just sit and talk about families or hobbies.

Myth 5: Fun Time at Work Will Compromise Results.

This is one of managers' largest concerns. Somehow many of them feel that every minute spent chuckling is a minute lost toward bottom-line results.

Alas

Somehow three of us stepped out of our offices at the same time, met in the hallway, and began chatting. I don't even remember what we began laughing about, but all three of us were really laughing (not very quietly). Our boss stepped out of his office with a furious, red-faced look and said, "Is this what I'm paying you for?" We were embarrassed, humiliated, and angry. I left the company shortly after that, as did the other two people. It was a stifling environment where fun was not allowed. Ten years later, I still remember that incident.

—Retail sales manager

Fun-loving environments are actually more productive than their humorless counterparts. A fun break can reenergize your employees and ready them for the next concentrated effort. In one Microsoft group, employees take breaks whenever they want by surfing the Web or playing games on their computers. They say that these playful activities clear their minds so that when they return to the project at hand, they are fresher and sharper.

We have a tradition of celebrating birthdays. We recently celebrated the birthday of our financial officer with a special morning tea. We always sing happy birthday, share a funny story or two, and chat over tea and cake. Yes, it's a chunk of time out of the morning, but we've had a few laughs, our financial officer has been valued (and he truly is!), and everybody goes back to work.

—Matt Hawkins, New Zealand ministry

You might be thinking, "If I allow my employees to surf the Web or celebrate birthdays during work, they will never get their work done." Maybe you believe that only exceptional employees can be trusted to that degree. The secret to allowing fun at work is to be *crystal-clear* with your employees about their performance goals. Co-create measurable and specific goals with them; then evaluate their performance using those goals.

Some of the most productive, successful organizations in the world are renowned for fun. Southwest Airlines chairman of the board Herb Kelleher set the famous Southwest tone. He has loaded baggage on Thanksgiving Day, ridden his Harley-Davidson motorcycle into company headquarters, and golfed at the Southwest golf tournament with just one club. He even arm-wrestled another CEO for the rights to an advertising slogan.

Southwest flight attendants get their kicks by singing the departure instructions to their passengers. All this fun and they still get results. On January 24, 2013, Southwest proudly announced 40 consecutive years of profitability, a record unmatched in commercial airline history. They're also ranked first in America's Happiest Airlines for Holiday Travel by *Forbes* for the third consecutive year and one of the Five Most Likeable Companies of 2012 by Likeable Media. Finally, they were recognized by Glassdoor.com as the Employees Choice Awards Best Place to Work 2013.[26]

> *If you aren't having fun in your work, fix the problem before it becomes serious: ask for help if you need it. If you can't fix it and won't ask for help, please go away before you spoil the fun for the rest of us.*
>
> —*Russ Walden*

Myth 6: You Have to Have a Good Sense of Humor (or Be Funny) to Create a Fun Work Environment.

Some of you aren't funny. Well, you aren't. And that's okay. Many terrific bosses are not necessarily funny (or even very fun-loving). In many cases, they simply allow others' humor and playfulness to come out. They support rather than create fun at work. Let others initiate the kicks if fun is not your strength.

> *Our national director recently did something very unusual (for him) at our monthly strategy meeting. He asked each of us whether we preferred Coke or Pepsi. Depending on our answer, he pulled a Coke or Pepsi out of this bag. He never does things like that. It was a riot!!*
>
> —*Employee from a nonprofit organization in Russia*

You might bring fun into your workplace by having brown bag lunches with interesting speakers and topics. During a hobby-sharing lunch, one employee took everyone to a local park to demonstrate his remote-controlled airplanes. Another brought a local merchant to give a session on wine tasting. Another invited the local golf pro to give everyone a lesson.

Fun is a state of mind. Leaders can create this state of mind—but to do so, they must care about people, show trust and appreciation, be humble enough to join in and believe it is a good use of time! Joy is the lasting by-product of having fun and being with folks that give you energy. Leaders can bring joy to people's lives, even when things are tough. Creating a sense of being a part of something very special is the key.

—President of a major airline company

Bottom Line

Experience in companies of all sizes proves it: fun enhances creativity, fosters commitment, improves morale, mends conflicts, and creates effective customer relationships. It enhances workplace productivity when work goals are clear. Let fun happen. That fun will energize, motivate, and keep talented people on your team.

TWELVE

CREATE CONNECTIONS

Ponder this: Is your organization easy to leave?

It's *easy* to leave a workplace

- Where you feel no connection.

- Where you have no group of colleagues who can offer support, information, or plain old gripe sessions.

- If it is difficult to move your ideas through the pipeline.

- If you do not have relationships that help you get your work done.

- If you don't look forward to seeing the people with whom you interact.

- If you don't feel proud of or don't understand the organization's mission and purpose.

It's *difficult* to leave a workplace when you have links (connections, relationships, ties, associations). On some level you know that's true. But are you helping your talented people create the links that will engage and retain them?

Are You a Linker or Nonlinker?

A *nonlinker* thinks, "If I link my employees to other functions or departments, someone there will steal them."

A *linker* thinks, "If I don't link my employees to other functions or departments, their knowledge and skills are less likely to grow. My employees' productivity will be limited to the resources of their own department. Their work may become too function focused for overall success, and I won't be as connected as I need to be, either."

> Just as we are all at the center of our own particular universe, we are also at the center of our network. We realize, of course, that all the other people are at the center of their networks, and that is how it should be. Each of the people in this network serves as a source of support (referrals, help, information) for everyone else in that network. Those who know how to use the tremendous strength of a network realize this very important fact: We are not dependent on each other; nor are we independent of each other; we are all interdependent with each other.
>
> —*Bob Burg, author of* Endless Referrals

To increase performance *and* retention, consider how you can support links between your employees and three important factors. What can you do to link your employees to

- People?

- Purpose?

- Profession?

Link to People

Do you have a best friend at work? What a strange question to ask. (Especially in some countries and cultures.) What does the answer have to do with employee engagement or retention? According to Gallup, a lot![27] Research shows that strong relationships at work are absolutely key to retaining your people and key to their productivity. In fact, most of us want and need colleagues to think with, work with, and create with.

An overwhelming majority of American employees perceive a strong link between their workplace productivity and the quality of their personal relationships with co-workers, suppliers and company alumni, according to a survey by SelectMinds, a leader in Corporate Social Networking. In fact, 87 percent of all employees say they are most productive in their jobs when surrounded by colleagues with whom they have a good relationship/rapport.[28]

Alas

The competition offered me a 10 percent salary increase, and I took it. My boss was blown away by my resignation. He thought I loved my job and had no idea that I could be enticed away. So what grabbed me?

Frankly, it was a combination of things. I felt no real connection to my workplace or the team. Maybe if we had spent a little more time together, or I had felt more a part of things there, I might have stayed. The company I'm joining operates primarily in teams. I'm hoping that will provide more of the interaction that I'm looking for. So the money was attractive, but the chance to be part of a team mattered even more.

—Engineer, aerospace firm

Most workers want to be linked to a group of people with whom they enjoy working. In fact, for the newest generation entering the workforce, the number one question on their minds may be, Will I work with a team I like?

This is so true that they will even leave together. We heard recently of 13 IT employees resigning as a group!

Work atmosphere is the main reason I stay. We have an amazing teamwork philosophy. In fact, it doesn't matter where in the country I am. I can stop at any retail dealership and say, "Hi, I'm a fuel service engineer," and I'm immediately welcomed. It feels great to be part of a family like that.

—*Gas station owner*

Encourage your employees to build their networks by joining (or starting) professional and social groups inside your organization. You've probably heard of affinity groups and employee or business resource groups (ERGs or BRGs). One global organization proudly boasts 54 ERGs! Here are just a few we've heard of:

- Gender, racial, ethnic groups
- Young professionals
- Veterans
- Non–US born
- Faith based
- Gays, lesbian, bisexual, transgender, and allies
- Parents or work/life
- Early career
- People with disabilities
- Intergenerational
- Women in leadership
- New employees
- Pet owners
- Gen Ys
- Curly-haired people (not kidding!)

You name it, it exists somewhere, in an organization led by managers smart enough to know the value of linking!

In Asia, many organizations have "Friends@Work," social recreation committees that plan social events for employees. These are funded by the company to help build relationships. They also have volunteer committees, where employees get together for an outing with the elderly, handicapped or disadvantaged children. This links them to the community and to one another.

Supporting connections with people throughout your organization can help you attract and keep prized employees. Some ideas:

To Do

★ Use your company intranet to help boost team collaboration, find organizational resources, and acknowledge and celebrate successes.

★ Reinstate *lunch*. (Kudos to you if it still exists in your organization.) Encourage people to enjoy it together.

★ Encourage teams, task forces, and ERGs, where people form new links and new friendships. Sponsor a departmental sports team, or have sports outings with other departments or companies.

★ Have family events—picnics, bring the kids to work day, bring your dogs to work day.

But what if you work in London and your team is in Kansas? Hundreds of thousands of employees and their bosses work in virtual environments. They've created dozens of ways of building and maintaining their relationships, despite geographic differences. Here are some of the ways they link people, get work done, have some fun, and hang on to talent:

To Do

★ Hold virtual town hall meetings, where employees interact with management via video conferencing.

★ Find internal social media platforms, where people can form groups to share pictures, favorite recipes, or stories.

★ Check out chat rooms and bulletin boards, where subject matter experts give employees instant answers.

★ Hold good old-fashioned conferences, once a year, where people physically come together in one place at one time!

Link to Purpose

No matter what business you're in, everyone in the organization needs to know why.

—*Frances Hesselbein, CEO, Leader to Leader Institute*

You don't need to work for the American Red Cross or The Bill Gates Foundation to build a meaningful connection between an employee and the organization. According to a report by global brand consultancy Calling Brands, corporate purpose is emerging as a powerful driver of attraction, retention and productivity. "The survey revealed that, on average, 57% of respondents (64% Germany, 58% US, 48% UK) said they would favor joining an organization that has a clearly defined purpose. Moreover, an average of 65% claimed that purpose would motivate them to go the 'extra mile' in their jobs and 64% claimed it would engender a greater sense of loyalty towards the organization they work for. Purpose will be increasingly recognized by corporations as an important driver of engagement."[29]

As a manager, you can do a lot to create the link. Sometimes all it takes is a discussion about the history of the company, its founders, its reason for being, the important needs it meets, or what customers say the company has done for them through its product line or service.

One medical device manufacturer brought in patients from a local hospital whose lives were saved or enhanced thanks to the company's product. All employees at all levels attended these meetings and were able to ask questions of these users. Employees swelled with pride and deepened their link to the organization.

Meetings with the president, CEO, or other senior leaders are critical to linking employees with an organization's purpose. While mission statements capture the underlying principles of the organization and seldom change, the goals of the organization are dynamic. Keep employees abreast of these organization-wide changes to help them feel connected.

How do you create a strong link between your talented people and the organization and its purpose? There are many ways:

To Do

★ Have regular open forum meetings. If employees feel they are being heard, they will feel a stronger connection to you and the group. Allow diverse opinions and disagreement on the way to finding solutions that work.

★ Encourage group outings regularly, and don't expect people to do this on their own time. Consider allowing one paid afternoon per month—as long as it's a team activity.

★ Give employees time to talk. Managers are often so worried about work not getting done that they discourage personal conversations among their staff. What they don't seem to understand is that these conversations help employees feel connected to each other. And ironically, they're often talking about work!

★ Host informal breakfasts or lunches. Your department needs to make informal connections occasionally. In a semisocial atmosphere, you can introduce a new project, get creative juices flowing, or just kick off a new month. One senior manager in a public relations firm gave $25 lunch coupons to the 60 employees in his unit three times a year. There was only one instruction each time: "Take someone you don't know well to lunch, and learn more about them and the work they do." Smart linking!

★ List all the interdepartmental meetings you attend in a week. (Does the list give you a headache?) Which ones could you delegate to members of your team? The linking could be great for them and freeing for you.

Purpose Beyond the Organization

Getting your employees involved in community service can help them feel linked. For some, these activities are a major reason for choosing one organization over the next or staying with their present one. According to a PricewaterhouseCoopers study, "88% of graduate students and young professionals factor an employer's Corporate Social Responsibility (CSR) rating into their job decision. And 86% would consider leaving a job if their employer's CSR performance no longer held up."[30]

Don't despair if your organization is not yet involved in socially responsible activities in the community. You can support community projects your employees are involved in. Or you might build your own. Either way, promoting a cause within your department or company gives employees a sense of pride, promotes teamwork, fosters a bond among employees, and provides skill development as well. Companies have involved their employees in classrooms, community centers, charity runs, bicycle tours, public housing projects, outreach to the elderly, and many other life-changing activities.

Every year, my company sponsors several hundred cyclists in a ride called the Best Buddies Challenge. My colleagues and I train for months for this event, have a wonderful time doing it and help raise millions of dollars for the charity. The best part of it all is knowing we've supported a global volunteer movement that creates opportunities for one-to-one friendships, employment and leadership development for people with intellectual and developmental disabilities. I'm proud to be a part of a company that supports community activities like this one!

—Staffing director, investment bank

If you're wondering what you might do to support this kind of purpose, consider these possibilities.

To Do

★ Investigate local projects, discuss at a staff meeting, and ask who's interested.

★ Ask employees to suggest projects, and select one or two (or more) a year to work on as a group.

★ Invite several local volunteer groups to describe what they are doing in the community, and encourage your team to volunteer together.

★ Invite another department to join with you on a local community project (great networking for your employees).

Link to the Profession

Professional communities exist inside and outside the organization. On the outside, associations give people a chance to learn what is happening elsewhere. Conferences, trade shows, seminars, webinars, and online networking sites are also great ways to discover how other professionals handle similar problems and pressures. What unique approaches are working in other organizations? Often people come away from these meetings with renewed pride in their profession and new ideas to bring home to their organization.

The nonlinker's fear is that employees at a professional meeting might think the grass is greener elsewhere. What if they get job offers? What if their association interests pull them farther away from the job? All are possible. But all this is still possible *even if* you don't support their involvement. Your employees' loyalty level could spike, simply because you encouraged them to build these outside links.

Consider linking your talented people with communities of practice (CoPs) in their profession. CoPs exist online, such as within discussion boards and newsgroups, or in real life, such as in cafés, living rooms, field settings or factory floors. In CoPs, groups of people who share a craft and/or a profession come together with the goal of gaining knowledge related to their field. They share information and experiences with the group, learn from each other, and have an opportunity to develop themselves personally and professionally.

Here are some things you might do to help support and build professional connections for your team:

To Do

★ Offer paid memberships in professional associations as a reward for work well done.

★ Set aside time at staff meetings for your team to report on conferences or events they attend.

★ Offer to bring several of your people with you to your meetings.

★ Offer to speak at one of their association meetings.

★ Ask your employees (again) what groups they'd like to join or *start*, right here in your organization.

You can't build these connections *for* your employees. But you can be a role model. And you can encourage and reward the links they make.

Teach Them to Link

Start by asking what they want or need. When they look at you with a "what do you mean?" look on their faces, show them this list:

To Do

Ask employees whether they would like to

★ Get straight feedback.

★ Learn a specific skill.

★ Hear about opportunities.

★ Get information.

★ Get help with an idea.

★ Get a specific job.

★ Gain visibility.

★ Find new contacts.

★ Help more or give more.

Then ask yourself who—inside or outside your organization—could meet that employee's needs. Help them make the match—then watch linking work!

GO TO

Mentor
page 120

Let Them In on the Secret of Reciprocity

A long list of names is meaningless unless it represents real relationships, developed by offering your own help and input over time. Then, when the day comes that you need a job lead, a problem-solving tip, or just the inside scoop on the new boss, you'll be in the loop, not banished to the outer circle.[31]

The Latin expression *quid pro quo* means "something for something" or, in a more contemporary translation, "If you do something for me, I'll do something for you." If linking is only used to ask something of others, it will become one-sided and self-serving.

We often hear stories of "elegant currencies"—things you can offer that are easy for you to do that the other person needs but lacks resources to do. For example, you can teach somebody a new computer program. You can tell someone about a book you've read that could be invaluable to his or her work or even summarize it for him or her. There are so many ways that people can offer something in return.

To Do

Quid Pro Quo Menu. Services you can offer to your "links" in return:

Service	Example
Introduce links to others	A potential client or supplier
Provide original ideas	A new way to process orders
Help others brainstorm	Creative new ways to market a product
Volunteer help	At another's charitable event
Increase others' networks	Provide names of contacts another needs
Reduce others' workloads	Offer to help write part of a proposal
Offer feedback	Suggest ways to improve the marketing brochure
Recommend to others	Market product by word of mouth
Share expertise	Computer skills

Direct reciprocity doesn't have to be the only way this works. A hit movie based on the book *Pay It Forward* suggested that individuals offer to "give back" by giving to three other people. Eventually, we'd all win. Imagine an organization that plays out this philosophy. Perhaps you could begin this in your own department. Ask your employees how they can pay it forward to colleagues, to their profession, to their community, to their organization, perhaps even to their industry.

Bottom Line

Connections are a major reason people say they stay with organizations. If links are weak or nonexistent, disengaging or leaving is easier. Today's knowledge workers need to link to others to get their jobs done. Their links will strengthen yours—in the perfect *quid pro quo*—and they'll be more likely to stay.

THIRTEEN

BE ONE

Ponder this: What are they learning from you?

People with mentors are twice as likely to stay. And they won't just stay longer, they'll produce more.

Senior executives and human resource professionals know this. That's why mentoring programs around the globe have doubled in numbers in recent years. Companies that want to retain high-performing women and minorities are investing in mentoring programs; some believe good mentoring will break the glass ceiling. Mentoring has become a way not only to transfer crucial skills and knowledge but to inspire loyalty in new employees, emerging leaders, and older workers who might otherwise leave sooner.

Given the hierarchical structure of many Asian cultures, there are already semblances of mentoring in place. The seniors are expected to teach the juniors the ropes while the juniors are expected to obey and learn well so that they can, in turn, teach the next set of juniors.

—Wendy Tan, co-founder Flame Center

Companies are giving creative incentives to mentors, pairing mentors with new hires, and offering group mentoring and online mentoring to hasten the development of management and technical skills. They're even linking diverse cultures by pairing mentors with their mentees across the globe.

But this book is not about structured mentoring programs that HR professionals put in place. This is about the mentoring that *you* can do, from your position as a manager, now. And, it's not that complex. The more you act like a mentor to your direct reports, the more engaged they'll be. The more engaged they are, the less they'll think about leaving.

Weeks into his new job as a nurse manager, Robert faced a supervisor's nightmare: he had to fire a problem employee. "I kept calling on Charlotte. She walked me through it," says Robert, who at 29 was promoted from staff nurse to nurse manager at a prominent hospital in Miami. He found himself now managing former colleagues, nearly all female and many of whom were older and more experienced nurses. What helped him navigate potential pitfalls was his informal mentoring relationship with Charlotte, another nurse manager who had been with the hospital for 35 years. "Even if you've been a nurse for a long time, when you step into management it's a new role," she said. "You don't need a mentor to ask medical questions. You need to know how to swim in office politics." She guided Robert in how to deal with his difficult employee, how to document the turnaround steps he was taking, and ultimately, how to follow hospital policy in terminating the employee. "It's the toughest thing you'll do," she warned him. "Have your ducks in a row."

So What's a Mentor to Do?

Mentoring does not require specific training or a great deal of time. Every good manager mentors naturally, often without even realizing it. Here is a simple way to remember the art and science of mentoring and a template for you to use as you strive to improve your own day-to-day mentoring.

Model	Walk the talk. Model what you want your employees to do. Help them find other good role models as well.
Encourage	Find out where they need more support—then give it. Cheer them on, in good times and bad.
Nurture	Show you care about them and their unique skills and capabilities. Nurture their ideas, relationships, and them!
Teach **O**rganizational **R**eality	Tell it like it is. Help them avoid those organizational minefields that are never written about in any policy manual.

Model—Walk Your Talk

An executive I coached said he encouraged his employees to have work/life balance—that it was crucial to their health, well-being, and job effectiveness. I asked him how he modeled that for his employees. There was dead silence on the phone. Finally, he admitted, "I guess I don't really model that." It turned out his car was the first one in the parking lot every day and the last one to leave. His family rarely saw him. What was the effect on his employees? They paid more attention to what he did than to what he said. It was clear to them that work/life balance was not—and should not be—a priority.

—Executive coach

So, how effectively are you modeling the behaviors you hope your employees will replicate? Harvard professor Rosabeth Moss Kanter says that modeling needs to be dynamic, not subtle. "Dynamic modeling means you act as an obvious prototype for the protégé. It requires 'Follow me!' behavior that is obvious and noticeable."

If you want employees to exhibit work/life balance, demonstrate how you do it, in obvious, consistent ways. If you hope they'll be better listeners, be a terrific listener every time you interact with them.

If you want your talented people to delegate more effectively, delegate more effectively to them. If you want them to be continuous learners, talk about the online course you're taking to improve your skills in a specific area. You get the point.

How are *you* modeling in a day-to-day way? Here are some ideas:

123
MENTOR
Be One

GO TO

Listen
page 107

To Do

★ Be aware of what you are modeling—is it what you hope to see them doing?

★ Point out other good role models. Choose people who are good at the very things your employees are trying to learn.

★ Be authentic. Let them see you handling good and bad situations, under positive conditions and poor ones.

★ Discuss what you're trying to model. Is it coming through? How might you improve?

Encourage—Just-in-Time

Encouragement truly is all in the eye of the perceiver. For example, an employee says, "He never encouraged me," while her manager says, "I encouraged her all the time." How can you encourage effectively?

Clearly, attention and retention go hand in hand.

My boss moves away from his computer and phone, to a small round table, for every one of our weekly conversations. I feel like the most important person on the planet. He listens, asks great questions, gives advice, takes his time—even though I know how busy he is. I'd follow this boss to the ends of the earth!

—Manager, global restaurant chain

Those who *have* been encouraged are more likely to stay and to bring their best to the team.

Some managers encourage naturally, through casual conversations. Here's one way of offering encouragement, just in time. It consists of three steps:

1. ***Recognize:*** Notice something.

2. ***Verbalize:*** Say something.

3. ***Mobilize:*** Do something.

GO TO
———
Careers
page 18

Any of the three steps will encourage, but all three combined are much more powerful. For example, Liliana gives a beautifully designed flyer to her manager and says, "I've been doing some fiddling with that new graphics program."

> ***Recognize.*** Manager: "Hmm, looks great. I didn't know you like this kind of stuff." *(Good)*

> ***Recognize and Verbalize.*** Manager: "This is really good. Is this something you'd like to do more of ?" *(Better)*

> ***Recognize, Verbalize, and Mobilize.*** Manager: "If you like this kind of work, why not let Marc in Graphics know, and while you're there, find out when he's offering his next graphics course." *(Best)*

Impromptu mentoring of this type is even more important if you have limited time to meet with employees. For many employees, these simple interactions will send a strong message that they matter.

To Do

★ Remember to encourage them when things don't go as well as planned. If you're there for them during the good times and bad, they'll trust you, perform for you and stick around a while longer.

★ Encourage risk taking that is essential to growth. Take the culture into account as you do this!

★ Cheer them on—give regular positive feedback—and developmental feedback, too.

Nurture—on the Run

Countless employees who have left their corporations say that their managers never stopped long enough to understand them or care about them.

Alas

From an interview with a senior-level manager in a high-tech company:

Interviewer: Did you ever have a mentor?

Manager: You bet. He was my manager. He really cared about me. He'd stop in all the time, ask me some great questions, get me to think about what I was doing and why. He gave me some great strokes and kept my juices flowing.

Interviewer: Do you do that for anyone?

Manager: No—I would like to, but we don't really have the time these days.

Mentoring takes time—but not a lot. Mainly, it takes a willingness to show another person that you genuinely care.

Nurture Ideas. When employees come to you with suggestions or ideas about how they might approach something differently, do you immediately say no? Do you kill an idea before it is even off the tongue? We hear that employees feel put down and turned down far more than their managers are aware. And that makes leaving easier. Instead, try listening to the entire idea, try playing with it as a "what if." Ask for more information. Sleep on it; mull it over. Think, "Isn't that interesting" *before* you think, "It will never work."

Nurture Relationships. Get to know your employees and give them every opportunity to get to know you.

A senior marketing vice president at a top ten Fortune 500 company commented that she wished managers in her organization would recognize how

GO TO
———
Links
page 107

important a relationship with them was to their people. "And I don't mean anything deep," she said. "It's the little things, like a cup of coffee together once in a while." Employees want to feel they count and are noticed. When they feel invisible, it's easy for them to leave.

Help your talented people build relationships with others in the organization, too. Those connections will help them get their work done and increase the odds they'll stay.

In organizations, real power is generated through relationships. The patterns of relationships and the capacities to form them are more important than tasks, functions, roles and positions.

—Meg Wheatley

To Do

★ Show you care about your talented people and their unique skills, talents, capabilities—even their personal lives.

★ Link them to others who can help them grow.

★ Listen to their ideas with an open mind. Think, "What if?" before you think, "No."

Teach Organizational Reality

Everyone knows at least one sad story of a technically brilliant employee with everything to offer who derailed because of political blunders, lack of interpersonal skills, or ignorance of the unwritten rules.

Countless corporate advice books suggest that academic brilliance alone does not lead to success. Daniel Goleman talks about EQ (emotional quotient—your ability to monitor your own and others' feelings).[32] Paul Stoltz refers to AQ (adversity quotient—your ability to deal with bad luck or plans gone wrong).[33] Others point to arrogance, insensitivity to others, or managing upward instead of down (focusing more on superiors than on direct reports) as career stoppers.

These experts also mention that career stoppers in one organization are not necessarily stoppers in another. Arrogance might derail a talented employee on your team, while it's seen as a success factor somewhere else. The key here is to help your employees learn what works (and what doesn't) in *this* organization. Your ability and willingness to *tell it like it is* can save a career, perhaps for the benefit of your own organization.

Alas

She was technically brilliant. She graduated in the top 2 percent of her class in one of the top schools in the country. She was pursued by all of our competitors. We won. We offered opportunities for her to continue on her fast track, to work with other brilliant colleagues, to sit on a variety of committees that made decisions on our future direction. We had great plans for her.

She was so quick, though, that she started to rub people the wrong way. She continually ignored our chain of command. She stepped on toes. No one gave her any alternative ways to deal with the folks whose respect she needed.

Slowly, her influence eroded. Although she continued to be way out there in terms of what she knew, she just couldn't manage to communicate with her team or her peers. People avoided her. She became more and more isolated. And she became more and more unhappy with our organization. Before we knew enough to try to talk it out and give her some help, we lost her.

—Manager, high-tech company

Her style and interpersonal skills might have worked just great in school or even in another organization. They didn't work here, given this company's culture. And no one told her.

GO TO

Truth
page 196

Good mentoring can mean telling an employee that her actions could derail her in this company. Listen to the voice in your head that says, "That behavior isn't going to work here." It can also mean telling her which meetings she dare not be late for—or which managers she dare not go around. It's sharing news about the unwritten rules. About how the organization looks to you and how it behaves—often.

But what if you coach someone about organization politics and you are wrong? Your view is just your view. Could you mess it up even more? We don't think so.

We have never heard of a manager who mentored too much and thereby lost an employee. We've never heard of a manager who coached too often and thereby lost someone's trust. We've never heard of a manager who talked too frequently about how he or she saw the organizational world and failed to retain talent for that reason.

Employees need to know your point of view. They want to know your take on how people get and give resources, what kinds of influence strategies work and don't work, and what certain senior leaders want and don't want in their reports, their presentations, and their meetings. And they want to know this before they walk into a minefield. At the very least, they want to be able to look at something that didn't work and understand why!

So if you are nodding your head, consider using one of your own staff meetings to open a dialogue on organizational reality.

To Do

Invite your team to talk about any of the following topics:

★ What have I learned about what counts in this organization?

★ How have my failures and successes contributed to my growth?

★ What most surprised me about the culture?

★ What was the most difficult culture shift for me to make?

★ What are the ways to get in really hot water here?

★ How do people derail themselves?

★ What do I know now that I wish I had known then?

People have a hunger for frank conversation in organizations today. Because of the intense competition, few employees feel that they can really express themselves or ask the questions that are on their minds. Most people claim they do not like playing politics. But because it's a reality of corporate life, a mentor watches out for a protégé's organizational well-being. A mentor educates and protects a protégé from stumbling.

Following a seminar, we received this letter from one of the participants:

My reason for writing is to share an anecdote about a mentor who made a difference in my career. We had spent weeks working together on the development plan for one of my stars. It took many calls, many lengthy discussions; there were many issues involved, but we worked with the star to design a plan that made sense.

But here's what stands out. When we finished the last discussion and agreed it would work, I looked at him and said, "Done." I remember slumping back in my chair and taking a deep, relief-filled breath. I was happy we had settled things and happy that we were able to work out a solution. But in addition to that, I looked around my desk and saw all the pending projects, briefing papers, and other things that were piling up and had all taken a back seat to the week's ordeal. And what I said was, "Boy, I'm glad that's over. Now we can get back to work."

He locked my eyes and said, "You just don't understand, Joe; this is our work. If we don't do this, we have nothing. This is our job."

Now there's a mentor.

Mentor in Reverse

What do you want to learn? Who, on your team (or beyond), can teach you how to use social media to your advantage? Who's a dynamite presenter who could teach you some platform skills? Who could help you become a more effective networker?

Let your people mentor you. Let them tell you what they know. Ask them to coach you about how you might be more effective. They'll feel valued and respected because you asked.

Bottom Line

Your employees want you to teach them the ropes, and they know their careers will suffer if you don't. They want you to tell your own stories. Your failures and your success stories provide valuable insights that just don't come in other ways. They want you to model the behaviors you expect from them. Managers who mentor establish great rapport with their employees and find that there is a strong payback in engagement and retention.

FOURTEEN

Numbers

RUN THEM

Ponder this: How much does it cost to lose them?

Imagine that you arrive at work one morning to the evidence of a burglary. A brand-new desktop computer has disappeared from an employee's desk. You call the building security office and the police. Then you launch your own investigation. You are determined to find out how this happened and who is responsible. You will not rest until the case is solved. And you immediately increase security measures—no more property will be lost.

Now think about the last time one of your most talented employees was stolen by the competition or just walked out your door. What kind of investigation did you launch? What measures did you implement to prevent it from happening again? Maybe the loss of this precious asset set off no alarm bells because no one ever really assessed the cost of losing talent. It doesn't take long to run the numbers. And you may be surprised.

Numbers and financial statements are the universal language of business. Front-line workers and senior managers alike understand them. We'll be speaking of U.S. dollars here, but many of our clients are counting in euros, pesos, pounds, rupees, or one of another 180-plus global currencies.

A major health care organization conservatively estimated the cost of "regrettable" turnover at $60 million in one year, while a Silicon Valley high-tech firm found its turnover costs to exceed $120 million per year.

★ ★ ★ ★ ★

We're not just losing good people; we're losing great people. Almost one in every five of the people who leave us voluntarily every year is a top performer. The cost of this turnover in lost productivity, paperwork, recruitment, and training is huge—it's in the tens of millions of dollars.

—*COO of an international bank*

A careful assessment of the numbers might just convince you to focus more sharply on retaining your talent.

What's the Price Tag?

You may think these dedicated, talented people who have been critical to your success are easily replaced. And yes, you might even find replacements at lower salaries. We hear this argument often, especially during periods of high unemployment when many good people are looking for work. Often, though, the managers who say this have simply not calculated the real costs of turnover. Most experts agree that replacing a key person on your staff will cost you two times that person's annual compensation. "Platinum" workers (highly skilled professionals) could easily cost you four to five times their annual salaries.

Alas

John was one of our most talented engineers and was responsible for inventing some of our key technology. After a phenomenally successful year, he expected some kind of reward or recognition from his boss. When nothing was offered (not even a thank you), he met with his boss and asked for a 15 percent raise (about $15,000). His boss immediately said, "Forget it!" John did and left the organization to join a competitor who was thrilled to pay him 30 percent more than he had been making. Some said, "Oh, well, we'll replace him within weeks."

Here's what actually happened:

- *We hired a headhunter for $40,000 to try to steal someone like John from a competitor.*

- *After a three-month search, we found five good candidates and flew them all in for interviews at a total cost of $5,000.*

- *We selected the new guy (after much wining, dining, and selling) and agreed to a sign-on bonus of $10,000 and a moving allowance of $25,000. His salary was negotiated at 25 percent above John's ($20,000 difference in the first year).*

So the bottom line in salary and expenses looked like about $100,000 to get the new guy in the door. But wait—that's not all.

- *Our competitor won John (including his brilliant brain and technical knowledge) and went on to win a multibillion-dollar contract that would have been ours.*

- *John's buddies all started looking around, and the company executives got wind of it. Senior leadership decided to give them a 15 percent raise for two years in a row (at a cost of $200,000).*

- *We lost two or three other key people to competitors. Their technical expertise went with them. Our cutting-edge technology leaked out the doors, and we made our competition stronger almost overnight.*

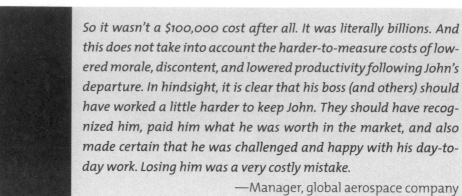

So it wasn't a $100,000 cost after all. It was literally billions. And this does not take into account the harder-to-measure costs of lowered morale, discontent, and lowered productivity following John's departure. In hindsight, it is clear that his boss (and others) should have worked a little harder to keep John. They should have recognized him, paid him what he was worth in the market, and also made certain that he was challenged and happy with his day-to-day work. Losing him was a very costly mistake.

—Manager, global aerospace company

This true story may seem unusual. Certainly not every employee is worth billions to your bottom line. However, no one, other than the manager in this story, ran the numbers to figure out what losing John actually cost. Managers seldom do, because then they would have to look for the real causes of turnover or find somewhere to place blame. They might even need to create retention strategies. Most leaders just don't want to do all that.

Some readers have reacted to this story by saying, "Hey, wait a minute. John left for more money. We thought you said it's seldom about money!"

Even in this story, his departure was not really about the money. It was about being heard, being appreciated, and being valued. John was hurt and frustrated by a boss who did not recognize or reward his efforts and who immediately dismissed his request for a raise. So what could John's boss have done differently? He could have

- Praised and thanked John for his major contributions.

- Listened to John's request and acknowledged that he was worth the raise—and that he would see what could be done and by when.

- Asked John what else he could do (if not an immediate raise) to reward him for his contributions.

- Calculated the cost of keeping John ($15,000) compared with the cost of losing him (you saw it—billions!).

GO TO

Ask
page 1

You will never really know what it costs to lose a talented employee if you never calculate the cost.

With the real cost of losing talent in mind, we recommend using the following table to assess the cost of replacing one of your excellent employees.[34] We have left blanks for you to add items that are relevant in your organization.

Run the Numbers

Item	Cost
Newspaper/Internet ads	_____
Search firm	_____
Referral bonuses	_____
Interview costs: airlines, hotels, meals, etc.	_____
Larger salary, sign-on bonus, or other perks	_____
Moving allowance	_____
Employee's lost productivity prior to leaving (disengagement; résumé update; time on Monster.com job searching; time spent interviewing, negotiating, and accepting new job)	_____
Manager's and team members' time spent interviewing	_____
Work put on hold until replacement is on board	_____
Overload on team, including overtime to get work done during selection and training of replacement	_____
Orientation and training time for replacement	_____
Lost customers	_____
Lost contracts or business	_____
Lowered morale and productivity	_____
Loss in business continuity across departmental boundaries and resulting lowered productivity	_____
Loss of other employees (They follow each other!)	_____
_____	_____
_____	_____

Item	Cost
_____	_____
_____	_____
Total estimated cost of losing one key employee	_____

Notice that some of these costs are *hard* and easy to measure (the first six on the list), while the remaining costs are *soft* and more difficult to measure, such as overload on the team and lost customers or business (opportunity costs). Ironically, some of the soft costs are the highest. Have you calculated those?

As part of a cost-cutting initiative, a boss told his department manager to let go of one of the department's four associates. The manager took some time to decide which person to cut, since they all had the same job responsibilities. Finally, he selected the poorest performer. But before he informed the unfortunate person, the best-performing, most experienced associate resigned. The manager was relieved because he was spared dismissing anyone. The manager's boss was pleased because the head count had been reduced. Yet the story's ending is anything but happy. The productivity of the person who resigned was nearly five times greater than that of the one who would have been laid off.[35]

What If They "Quit" and Stay?

Have you ever had a job where you brought less than your full self to work every day? What did it cost your organization?

Gallup's ongoing research suggests that actively disengaged employees (those who aren't just unhappy but are busy acting out their unhappiness) cost the United States over $300 billion a year in lost productivity. And research by Towers Watson, The Conference Board, and Bain Consulting supports those findings.[36]

So, while we know that physical turnover costs you a bundle, we now know, too, that psychological turnover can cost as much or more.

The good news is that what engages people also keeps them.

Consider this:

- How much money would your organization save if it reduced regrettable turnover by 1 percent? How would your organization use those dollars if it did not have to be spent on recruiting, hiring, and training new employees?

  We ran the numbers. We would save $91 million by reducing regrettable turnover by 1 percent. We'd been talking about how much we (store managers) all wanted the latest high-tech copy machine, but the $200,000 price tag made it a dream, not a possibility. We laughed when one manager did the calculation and announced we could buy 455 of these machines (plenty to go around) if we could just hang on to our talent!
  —FedEx Office Print & Ship Center, management meeting

- How much could your organization make if talented people brought 5 percent more of their hearts and heads to work? What could you do with that money?

Bottom Line

Run the numbers. Calculate the costs of losing and replacing key talent. Assessing these costs can be eye-opening for managers with an "easy come, easy go" attitude toward turnover. Sharpen your commitment to keeping your most valuable employees fully engaged and on your team.

FIFTEEN

Opportunities

MINE THEM

Ponder this: Will they find the next opportunity inside or out-side your organization?

What does this say?

OPPORTUNITY ISNOWHERE

The optimists among you read, *Opportunity is now here*!

The pessimists see, *Opportunity is nowhere.*

Still others of you are pretty sure it says, *Opportunity I snow here* (and we'd like to meet with you later . . .).

While this exercise usually brings a chuckle, it also underscores the truth about your employees and their perceptions about what's possible in your organization. Some scan the horizon and see absolutely no opportunities to learn or grow or be challenged. Others scan the same horizon and see an opportunity-rich environment. They envision possibility where others see nothing. What accounts for the difference? Often, *it's the manager.*

Love 'em managers help their talented people find opportunities inside the organization. These engagement-focused managers learn how to "opportunity mine" with the people they count on to stay and to bring their best to work every single day.

Lynne was a rising star, destined to do great things for the team— and her excellent work always made her supervisor look terrific. When she gave notice and her manager asked why, she answered, "I've been very happy here. You're a fantastic boss and the people are wonderful. It's just that I'm ready for something new, and this opportunity popped up in another company. I wasn't really looking for it; it just happened. I've decided to go for it."

The manager felt absolutely sick about losing her. What on earth would the team do? He offered more money, but the lure of this new, exciting opportunity had her already mentally and emotionally out the door. And when the manager probed a bit, he realized that the very opportunity she was leaving for was available within the organization.

Responsibility rests on both sides. She didn't ask, and her manager didn't offer to help her look for the next opportunity.

"I'm leaving for a better opportunity." That's the most common answer to the most popular exit interview question "Why are you leaving?" Sometimes it's just the politically savvy thing to say (rather than saying, "My boss was a jerk"), and sometimes it's the truth. Talented people have many choices about where they work. To keep them engaged and in your organization, learn how to "opportunity mine" with them.

Opportunity mining means opportunism in the most positive sense of the word. As the name suggests, it entails digging deeply, looking carefully, and ultimately capturing the new opportunity. Its three key behaviors are *seeking, seeing,* and *seizing.* As a manager, you can partner with your employees to opportunity mine. Begin by getting a feel for your own level of opportunity mindedness. Complete the Opportunity Audit to find out if you are *opportunity-high* or *opportunity-shy.*

Opportunity Audit

Using the following scale, jot down the number that best indicates the extent to which each statement is true for you:

1 = rarely; **2** = sometimes; **3** = usually; **4** = always.

I am at ease when considering other people's viewpoints. _____

I seek and use new technologies for improving productivity. _____

I know the trends in the marketplace; I could tell you what
competitors are doing and why. _____

I take an active role in professional group(s). _____

I network to help launch and support my career growth. _____

I am flexible about adjusting plans when the first or second
attempts at something fail. _____

I am quite comfortable interpreting the "gray" areas of policy
and practices. _____

I let my career interests be known through formal (job posting)
and informal (conversation) channels. _____

I know how to connect people and information, and others
seek my help in gaining access or information. _____

How did you do? If you are opportunity-high (scoring over 27), you are probably already seeking, seeing, and seizing opportunities for yourself and maybe even with and for your employees. If you scored on the low end (anything less than 18), you might benefit from the suggestions that follow.

Only the opportunity-minded manager can truly help employees find possibilities for themselves.

> *There is no security on this earth; there is only opportunity.*
> —*General Douglas MacArthur[37]*

Seeking Opportunities

People who seek opportunities often see the glint of something new—and can follow through for themselves *and* for their people. Your willingness to seek will model this positive action for your employees. *It's important for you as well.*

Do you ever ask employees about the types of opportunities they might be looking for and even help them look? (Yes, even if it means some good folks leave your team.)

> *One engineering firm is an opportunity-rich organization where managers are opportunity seekers. They have developed a culture where employees feel comfortable speaking up when they are getting bored or need or want a new challenge, a promotion, or a different type of work. Managers hold regular employee development meetings to discuss their employees' interests and desires. They surface new possibilities and link employee goals with opportunities that already exist or are on the horizon. After several years, the results are measurable and positive. Not only do they retain their talented people, but they also have enhanced recruitment, as interviewees see the company as an opportunity-rich organization.*

While this company launched their system-wide approach formally, you don't have to do it that way. You can do it yourself.

Hold development meetings with your employees. Your only topic should be their careers and what opportunities they might be seeking. "What if there are no opportunities here?" you ask. "And what if I simply cannot help them, or by opening the conversation, I encourage them to leave?" To answer these tough questions, put yourself in their shoes. How do you feel about a boss who wants to help you seek opportunities for yourself? What happens to your level of respect and commitment while you work for him or her? What happens to your sense of loyalty to this boss and even to the team or company? It all goes *up!*

To Do

★ Ask your employees what opportunities they seek. Help them think broadly and creatively, going beyond some of the first-blush responses such as a promotion. For example, ask what they'd like to learn this year.

GO TO

Enrich
page 37

Managers in an international hotel chain help their employees find opportunities to learn. One avenue is the company's Internet learning platform. The findings from a recent survey proved that giving employees the chance to build their skill sets via the online learning platform convinced them to stay. Forty percent of respondents believed that the chance to strengthen their skills was the primary factor for continuing their careers with the organization.

★ Brainstorm with them to surface opportunities to enrich the jobs they currently hold.

★ Check with managers in other departments to find out where new possibilities lie.

And remember: You won't see it 'til you seek it.

Seeing Opportunities

To discover opportunities, one must look at the world in a new way, through a new lens. It is impossible to make people smarter, but you can help them see with new eyes.

Turn back to the first page of this chapter. What did you see? Opportunity is now here? Opportunity is nowhere?

Most of us immediately lock on to one perspective and remain fairly confident in our findings. You may have chosen the first answer or the second and did not even consider the possibility that there is another point of view. Try this with your people. It is a great opener for a discussion of opportunities.

If you are an opportunity-minded manager, you will help your employees *seek* opportunities but will also help them to *see* those opportunities when they are right in front of their faces.

I can see how an important learning assignment a manager once gave me positioned me as an expert that others look up to. I was invisible before. I now understand how important it is for me to do the same for my direct reports.
—Manager, high-tech Zimbabwe firm

You can shed the right light, point out the features and distinctions, and turn the opportunity around or upside down to make it more visible. Best yet, you will teach your employees how to do those things for themselves. In partnership with your employees, ask, "Where and how carefully are we looking?"

A manufacturing company has an insiders' network of more than 360 people across the organization who are willing to take the time to talk with employees who want to learn about the nature of their work and the requirements of their jobs. This network has a computerized database (called Internal Information Interview Network) with the names and backgrounds of all the employees who participate.

Another organization we know of holds internal career fairs. The message to their talented people is that if they're looking for a new opportunity, they can look inside first!

What great ways to share information about opportunities. And what great ways to see if a pasture that looks greener on the other side of the fence really is greener. If your organization doesn't have databases or internal career fairs, you can still send folks who are wondering (and wandering) out to interview or e-mail people you know in other areas. Some managers let employees see by offering them the opportunity to fill in for others on vacation or sabbatical. Could you do this?

To Do

★ Look around to see what is changing in your department, division, or organization. What new projects are on the horizon?

★ Notice which department is expanding and which one is shrinking. There could be a perfect opportunity in a growing segment of your organization.

★ Who might be retiring soon or leaving for a new opportunity, opening up a possibility for one of your stars?

Seizing Opportunities

Many people are quite good at both seeking and seeing even camouflaged opportunities. But many of us are not so good at the most crucial behavior of the opportunity-minded person: seizing. For example, you may know someone who has a list of stocks or property she *almost* bought, a sport he *almost* learned, or a trip she *almost* took.

If you scored opportunity-high on the Opportunity Audit, you probably seek, see, and seize quite well. If you want to retain your top talent, help them learn to seize opportunities that come their way. What are the barriers to seizing opportunities? It may be helpful to figure out why your employees fail to act, and what you might do to help them.

To Do

★ If your employees do not create an action plan for their careers, help them analyze why they don't, and then help them do it. These plans should have action steps with time lines, potential obstacles, and support needed (what kind and by whom).

★ If your employees do not adhere to their plans (too busy, resources delayed), you could help them. Suggest regular meetings to discuss progress, and brainstorm solutions to obstacles.

★ If your employees second-guess themselves (analysis paralysis), you could help them avoid this pattern. With their agreement, point out second-guessing behaviors that are more apt to be delay tactics than true assessment. Again, with permission, push for action when they have done enough analysis.

★ If your employees decide a particular opportunity is just not for them, you could help them decide if it truly is not the right choice. After careful assessment, some opportunities are best passed by.

★ If your employees let others talk them out of it, you could help them be strong in the face of naysayers and risk-averse "friends" and colleagues. Those people may be opportunity-shy.

★ If your employees are just plain afraid to act, you could help them face the fear and just do it! Sometimes we just need an ally to provide support and courage when we get the jitters. Talk about the *what-ifs* with them—what if you try it and it doesn't work out? Usually the risks are not really life-threatening, even though they may feel like it.

There are two ways to get to the top of an oak tree. One way is to sit on an acorn and wait . . . the other way is to climb it.

Kemmons Wilson, founder, Holiday Inn Hotels

Bottom Line

Our research shows that, more than any other single factor, opportunities to be challenged, to do meaningful work, and to learn persuade people to stay.

If you hope to keep your talent on your team, you must become opportunity minded—an *opportunist* in the positive sense of the word—on behalf of your people. If they come to you wanting something new or something more, partner with them to find opportunities. Be glad that you have ambitious opportunity miners on your team. (Be glad they're not opportunity whiners—you know, constantly complaining about their lot in life.)

Be forewarned, too. If you can't help your best people seek, see, and seize opportunities at home, you will certainly lose them to organizations that can.

SIXTEEN

ENCOURAGE IT

Ponder this: Do you know what gets them up every morning?

What do your talented people love most about their jobs? And what are you doing to help them do more of the work they're passionate about and less of the work they dislike?

Passion for work means that people find what they do to be so exciting that it sometimes doesn't even feel like work—so exciting that it brings exhilaration, a "high." Granted, even those who have this passion seldom have it every day, but they do know that feeling, and they know when they lose it.

Choose a job you love, and you'll never have to work a day in your life.

—*Confucius*

People Are Passionate

Do you know what your employees are passionate about? When we asked dozens of people about their work passions, here is some of what we heard:

- "I love creating something new, something no one has ever seen or even imagined before."

- "I get a kick out of working on such an elite team. There is so much brilliance here."

- "I love drawing, welding, building something."

- "I love numbers. I'd rather work with them than with people."

- "I really get excited when I discover a new rule in math."

- "I love to help someone get better at something and get happier in the process."

- "I love managing others. What a kick it is to motivate and guide a team to do great things."

- "My passion is turnaround—taking something that is broken and fixing it."

- "I love being part of a great company that is doing important work."

A common theme surfaces among these diverse answers: When people are doing what they love, they are at their best. If you help connect your employees' passions to their jobs, you and they will reap the rewards.

Passions are wired into the real world more directly than our workday routines are. If you love something, you'll bring so much of yourself to it that it will create your future.

—Francis Ford Coppola

Uncover and Discover

So what can you do to help people find work that engages them deeply? First, ask. Ask several ways because people respond differently to different words. Try, "What work do you really love to do?" or "What are you passionate about?" or "What gives you the greatest thrill or kicks at work?" or "Are you doing what you choose to do?" (This question came from a colleague in Singapore, where the word *passion* doesn't quite capture the concept.)

GO TO

Ask
page 1

As they answer, dig a little deeper. Then think creatively about how you might put their passions to work.

> *Each month, our country leaders meet virtually and brainstorm—the idea is to re-create the passion and fanaticism we had when everyone could sit around one table. Each leader is responsible for communicating what we've discussed to his or her group and for kindling their enthusiasm, too.*
> *—Founder, international pharmaceutical company*

When was the last time you pulled your team together to ask for their ideas and to encourage them to build on one another's creativity? When did you sit down with one of your own team members and think together? Employees love the opportunity to think aloud with their managers; they want to "blue sky" occasionally. Do you know who wants this most? Who is most nourished by this kind of interaction? Have you made time for it? Have you made time for them?

When one manager had the "passion conversation" with his employee, here is how it went:

Manager: *What do you love to do? What are you passionate about?*

Marta: *I've recently learned to use a new piece of graphic software, and I've created brochures for my church. I'm having a ball with it.*

Manager: *I wonder if there is a way we could use your talent and interest here at work.*

Marta:	I've been thinking about it and wondered if I could take on the layout of the new company newsletter we've been talking about.
Manager:	How would that work out with your current heavy workload?
Marta:	I will definitely get my work done. You know that about me. This project will be above and beyond my current workload.
Manager:	Let's give it a try. Keep me posted as you work on the first issue. Let me know what's working and what's not.

GO TO
_____
Enrich
page 37

Marta was feeling pretty bored with her job. She'd been doing the same work for years, and the thrill was gone. She had even been thinking of leaving. She poured herself into the new project, teamed with colleagues, and turned out a first-rate newsletter. Her teammates and boss praised her and were astounded at her accomplishment.

Since that event, Marta has expanded her job to include multiple graphic arts projects. Her boss worked with her to restructure her job so that some of her former duties went to other people. Marta's energy and productivity have soared, and she wakes up eager to go to work. The key to her renewed enthusiasm is that her boss collaborated with her to uncover and then capitalize on her passion.

What if passion lies outside work? Some people are more passionate about skiing or about their children than about their work. What do you do then? Think about how the workplace might allow them to do more of what they love. Telecommuting, flextime, and on-site daycare centers are all strategies that support people's passions.

> I can't imagine leaving this job. The day-to-day work is good and the team is great. But one of the best aspects of my job is that some of us go skiing most Fridays. We work hard all week to get the work done. We sometimes work evenings and even on the weekend when necessary. Then we take off. Skiing is my passion and this job allows me to enjoy it every week. How many of those jobs are there?
>
> —Accountant, software company

This highly productive employee will continue to produce for his boss and team. That's the payback for his manager's flexibility.

To Do

★ Ask your employees what they love to do. What are they passionate about?

★ Dig deeper. Ask for examples so you really understand what they are saying to you.

★ Get creative. Collaborate with them to find ways to either incorporate their passion into the work they do, or flex the work somehow to allow time for their passion outside work.

Passion Igniters

Most managers need a little help building passionate teams. Here are a few passion igniters to consider:

Hire for Passion

Why not select for passion in the first place? Find out if the candidate has a passion for making a difference or for your company's product or service. What about a passion for the work your unit does, or for working on a team? If you build a team of passionate people, they'll not only produce for you— they'll actually help retain each other.

Show *Your* Passion

Share the passion you have for the work with your team. Your actions model what you expect from others.

The leader of a fast-growing financial corporation spoke to his regional leaders at a recent conference. When he walked into the room, he received a thunderous standing ovation. His talk was about the challenges and successes of the company—and focused largely on the role of people in the success equation. Midway through his speech, he said, "It's all about product, processes, and people. Without the people, all we have is an empty building—nothing else." In his closing remarks, he said, "I love this company. And I love the people in it!" The place exploded.

This leader feels passionate about his work and the people he leads. And he's not afraid to show it.

Share a Meaningful Mission

What if you shifted from maximizing profit to maximizing purpose? What if you could help employees fall in love with your company's agenda?

Speaking of agenda—what is yours? Why does your team or organization exist? What is your mission? Share that mission with your employees. Then, clearly link employees' work to the mission. Tell them how their work contributes to it. Tell them how critical they are to you, to the mission of the team, and to the organization.

I've been the janitor and maintenance expert here for 30 years. We take care of older people who need nursing care and help with their daily living. They deserve the best after all they have done and given in their lives. I love my work. I help make this building beautiful and safe for the people who work here and the people who live here. The director here gave me an award for my service and told everyone how critical I am to serving our residents. That award hangs on my wall at home.

—Maintenance expert, nursing home

This man is crystal-clear about the value of his work. The mission of the organization is the reason for his being there, and it inspires him.

To Do

★ Hire passionate people for your team.

★ Share and show *your* passion for the work and for the people.

★ Articulate and link people to the mission of your organization or team.

Passion Busters

Sometimes the fire is there at the beginning, and it just plain goes out. People with passion can burn out if someone or something smothers their passion. They can also move to a place where their passion can be rekindled!

He loved training and teaching others and told me he wanted to do more of that. Every chance he had, he would volunteer to teach a class, any class, even if it wasn't technical training. He learned to facilitate a team-building process that proved to be very successful in his business unit. But I just couldn't free him up to do more of what he loved. He was one of our best engineers, and we couldn't afford to have him pulled off his key projects to do this other work. How silly, in hindsight, that I was so protective of him and his time—now I have neither. He left us six months ago for a job that lets him utilize his talent and passion.

—Director, public service organization

Organizational Constraints

Which organizational constraints prevent you from giving your employees different work or more of the kind of work they love? The list is often lengthy. Some people just call the constraints "reality." You might think that in reality we don't have enough of the following:

- Time—We barely have time to do our jobs, let alone help our people find work they love.

- Money—The organization just slashed budgets again. We have no money for extras.

- Staff—We laid off the human resources expert who helped me match employees to meaningful community outreach projects. I don't know how to make those links, even if I had the time.

- Management support—My manager is in the same spot I'm in: not enough time, money, or staff.

- _____ (fill in the blank)

GO TO

Question
page 157

These constraints may be real. But remember, if you don't help your talented employees find work they love in your organization, you will lose them. Do you have enough time, money, and staff to deal with their loss and replacement?

People Change

Think about it. Do you love the same things you loved 10 years ago? Or do you have some new passions?

Sometimes passion stops because people change. I have a collection of un-read books on topics I used to be very interested in—and am not now. Passion found another avenue for expression.

—_A reviewer for this book_

GO TO

Ask
page 1

This is why the "stay interview" is so important and why you need to have these conversations regularly, with anyone you hope to keep on your team. Their passions might change; and when the thrill is gone, they could be, too. Ask your talented people what's new. And then explore together what could be new!

Self-Interest

When you help your best employees uncover and pursue their passions, they may need to leave you to pursue those dreams. Out of self-interest (sometimes team interest), you might tend to avoid the passion discussion. Yet, your odds of keeping those people are better when you collaborate with them to find exciting, meaningful work right where they are.

> *My passion was the volunteer work I was doing in my community. I spent evenings and weekends with a group that was working with inner-city kids in Los Angeles. We were mentoring them and providing safe playgrounds and educational opportunities. At work I honestly just showed up, did the minimum, and then shot out of there at 5:00 p.m. sharp. I sat down with my boss one day and described the volunteer work I was doing and how much it meant to me. He had a brilliant idea. He said that his boss had told him that the organization was committing to some new community outreach programs and that they were thinking of creating a new role in the organization. The next thing I knew, I became the director of community projects for our corporation. My work and my passion are now one and the same. As long as I can do this, I will never leave this organization!*
>
> *—Director, entertainment company*

The boss lost this employee from the team (it was inevitable) but *saved* him—and his passion—for the organization.

To Do

★ Assess the organizational constraints that serve as passion busters. Are they real? How can you overcome them?

★ Be honest about your self-interests. Get clear about the costs and benefits of helping employees find work they love.

★ Support and encourage your employees as they change, grow and exhibit new passion.

In the closing remarks of his book *What Should I Do with My Life?* Po Bronson tells the story of being invited by Michael Dell of Dell Computer to participate on a panel at a gathering of the Business Council, a group of more than 100 CEOs from some of the biggest companies in the country. The panel was asked a great question: "What do employees want? What would it take to get more commitment out of them, more ideas out of them, more value out of them?"

Bronson answered this way:

They want to find work they're passionate about. Offering benefits and incentives are mere compromises. Educating people is important but not enough—far too many of our most educated people are operating at quarter-speed, unsure of their place in the world, contributing too little to the productive engine of modern civilization, still feeling like observers, like they haven't come close to living up to their potential. Our guidance needs to be better. We need to encourage people to find their sweet spot. Productivity explodes when people love what they do.[38]

Bottom Line

People who do what they love usually do it very well. If passion is missing at work, your best people may not bring their best *to* work. So collaborate with them to uncover and discover what they love to do. Link them and their work to your mission, and help them remove the barriers to doing what they love. You'll gain enthusiastic employees who will stay engaged and productive—and *on your team*.

★

SEVENTEEN

Question
RECONSIDER THE RULES

Ponder this: Which would you rather keep—
the rules or the people?

If innovation is so important, why is it so hard to support? Why is it so easy to say no before saying yes? Why is it easier to see if there is a precedent for what an employee wants to do?

When your employees come to you with new ideas, concepts, or rule breakers, they want to hear "You've got a point" or "Let's give it a try" or "Maybe that will work." They want you to (at least occasionally) go to bat for them—to truly advocate for the change they want.

They want you to recognize their good ideas and innovative solutions, and they want *you* to support their questioning. You will increase the odds of engaging and keeping talented employees if you allow them to question the rules about their jobs, the workplace, and even the business.

A Rule's a Rule

The world would be even more chaotic if there were no rules. We count on rules to provide safety and sanity in our communities and workplaces. Yet most of us would agree that progress demands questioning the rules.

What if these people hadn't questioned the rules?

- **Wright Brothers:** Why can't people fly?

- **Steve Jobs:** Why can't we create phones that are also computers?

- **Thomas Edison:** Why can't we light our homes with electricity?

- **Fred Smith:** Why can't we move packages across the globe overnight?

- **Jonas Salk:** Why can't we prevent polio?

What if others hadn't asked these questions?

- Why can't we go to the moon?

- Why can't we use lasers to perform surgery?

- Why can't we share data instantly over long distances?

- Why can't we build our social connections on line?

- Why can't we create radar-invisible aircraft and ships?

You get the idea. The rule questioners and ultimately the rule breakers are our innovators. They improve our lives, and they are the backbone of successful organizations.

Darren was a new employee, hired to bring us fresh ideas and an outside perspective. He began to annoy us during his first month. He kept asking us questions like "Have you thought about doing it this way?" and "Why does this process take eight steps, when it could be four?" We held firmly to the way it had been done—why fix it if it ain't broken? Darren hung in there for six months and then shocked us all by leaving. He said that new ideas were not appreciated here. The sad thing is he's right.

—Manager, global medical technology firm

You might be thinking that Darren could have waited for a few months before suggesting all those changes. But didn't they hire him for his fresh ideas? Darren would have thrived in a workplace that truly encourages creativity.

So how open are you to the questions your employees bring you?

To Do

Complete the following sentences to determine whether you are more like Manager A or Manager B:

★ When employees ask me to question the rules, I most often

Manager A

- ☐ Give them a quick yes or no answer.
- ☐ Give them the reasons why we do it this way.
- ☐ Tell them I don't have time to deal with it.
- ☐ Suggest they ask someone else.

Manager B

- ☐ Tell them I would like to explore it further with them.
- ☐ Avoid justifying how we currently do it.
- ☐ Suggest a time frame for dealing with their question.
- ☐ Collaborate with them to find other resources if necessary.

If you are more like Manager A, you may be action oriented and highly productive. While you may have many excellent traits, you also could be a *question-unfriendly manager*. It won't take long for your employees to recognize that and

- Stop bringing you questions.

- Shut down their creative, innovative brains.

- Become less enthusiastic about work (and possibly less productive, too).

- Leave you for a workplace where their questions are encouraged.

If you are more like Manager B, you may also be highly productive. But you tend to respond eagerly and openly to your employees' questions, and you are a *question-friendly manager*. You are used to thinking, "What if that worked?" or "Why not see if we could change that policy?" or "How could this idea make us more productive?" You spend time brainstorming with your employees, and you collaborate with them to find answers to their questions.

Think about the people who first asked about these policies:

- Job sharing

- Flextime

- Telecommuting

- Casual dress

- Self-managed teams

- Childcare centers

- Employee ownership plans

- Maternity/paternity leaves

These are just a few of the workplace innovations that many employees now take for granted. How would any of these ideas have been welcomed in your organization 10 years ago? How about today? If they are against the rules in your workplace, question the people who could change them.

A group of highly valued engineers from India had what some people heard as a couple of strange requests. They asked their manager to ask the senior engineering manager

- *To put carpet in their work area so they could take their shoes off and line them up against the wall, according to their custom, and*

- *To install a small kitchen so their wives could come in to cook their preferred Indian cuisine.*

There was no precedent for this request, and the policy manual certainly didn't support it. The senior engineering manager considered the cost ($5,000) and the gain (a very happy team) and said yes. He said it was the best $5,000 he's ever spent to motivate and retain a talented work group.

This team's manager had the courage to forward their request. And the senior manager had the foresight to listen, as well as the courage to act. Are you like these managers?

GO TO
_____

Space
page 183

Please Hold Your Questions Until the End

How many times have you heard that? Usually there is no time for the questions. Or the speaker didn't really want questions. If you are a question-friendly manager, you welcome employee questions and innovative thoughts at any time, in any amount, and on any topic.

A question not asked is a door not opened.
—*Marilee Adams, author of* Change Your Questions, Change Your Life

Imagine the talent that is lost (often to the competitor) because no one took the time to listen to the challenging questions of innovative people.

He was always too busy, and we knew we shouldn't bother him with questions or new ideas about our processes. He liked to work by the book, and he wanted us to follow the rules and just get it done. The sad thing was, our team came up with a better, faster way to turn out a superior product. We knew that if they were ever given a chance, our ideas could make money for the company. We kept our mouths shut and just kept working. I left the company and found a more innovative place to work.

—Supervisor, manufacturing team

An executive in China said that questioning is harder to do there, given the traditional education system that emphasizes knowing facts and answers. She said that you need to consider how to question safely, without causing political repercussions.

If you manage in an environment where questioning the rules is foreign and even risky, find mentors who can help you gently shift mindsets and practices that have prevented rule questioning in the past. Your employees will thank you for trying!

Too Much of a Good Thing: Rules, Guidelines, Policies, Procedures

All are necessary to some degree, especially to effectively operate large, complex organizations. But the rules often take on a life of their own. They multiply, they live in huge manuals, and they begin to stifle productivity and creativity. One team jokingly called themselves a "ship of rules."

Serena: *Did you know that this approval form to spend $30 came back to me after three weeks in the organization with 15 signatures, including the CFO's?*

Boss: *Why on Earth would it take all of that ridiculous time and effort?*

Serena: *It's the rule.*

Boss: *Let's see what we can do to break that one!*

Reengineering (a process widely used in the 1990s) was all about tearing down those restrictive rules. Many organizations literally started with a blank sheet of paper and created brand-new processes, usually with fewer rules and steps. One hospital pulled all its employees into a large meeting room to examine the way they were doing the work. They had a mock patient enter their system. She and her paperwork moved around the room and met with people representing admissions, diagnosis, referral, and treatment. Every stop represented the accepted rule and step for either the patient or her paperwork. The exercise revealed (to the horror of everyone) that one patient and her paperwork had made 50 stops through a bureaucratic maze before she began treatment.

Overgrown rules sometimes need questioning. If your talented employees get bogged down in them, they will spend too much time navigating the bureaucracy, not to mention filling out paperwork. They will spend too little time innovating and creating new solutions, services, or products. They will also look for an opportunity to work elsewhere, in a freer workplace with fewer rules and restrictions.

In Russia there is a saying: rules are meant to be gotten around (not broken). This is challenging for those of us involved in making the rules. However, I have noticed that there is nothing quite so deflating as telling someone what the policy says.

—*Manager with PepsiCo, Russia*

To Do

★ Encourage your employees' questions. Let them know that any time is a good time to ask.

★ Support your employees' attempts to reduce the number of rules in your organization. Suggest they form a *silly rules committee* to stamp out rules that are—you got it—silly.

★ Hold regular rule-busting meetings just to look at rules, systems, and procedures that no longer work. Put different employees in charge of each meeting. Fight for the reexamination of a rule you *know* needs to go!

Are You Boxed In?

You have no doubt been asked (probably more than once) to think "outside the box." How ironic that most managers feel like the box has been handed to them (often by their bosses) and that they are supposed to think and act inside it. The box typically feels fairly rigid, as if it were made up of concrete walls—the rules. But with a shift in thinking, your box can be composed of different materials, each with unique properties. Here is an example:

This box has walls made of four materials.

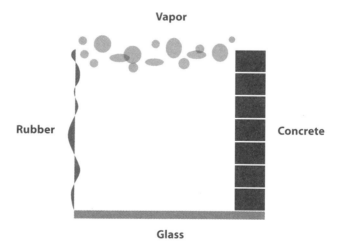

- **Concrete.** This wall represents rules that are truly rigid. It cannot be broken, pushed, bent, or shattered. *"You must have a medical degree to practice medicine in this hospital."*

- *Glass.* This wall is strong and sturdy, but if you hit it just the right way with just the right instrument at the right time, it will break. It represents the rules that may seem unbreakable but actually can be broken. *"A woman will never be CEO of a major corporation."*

- *Rubber.* This wall is thick and strong, but it has some give to it if you are willing to push hard. It represents rules that might be pliable. *"We all put in a 40-hour week, from eight to five, five days a week."*

- *Vapor.* This wall is made up of our beliefs, assumptions, and perceptions about the rules. *"People will never fly."*

If you examine the rules you operate by, you will find that few of them are truly concrete. They just feel that way. The most formidable aspect of the box is often the vapor wall. Your beliefs and assumptions—or the company's—often prevent you from questioning the rules. They may also keep you from hearing your employees' questions.

> *SportsMind is an organization that specializes in experiential learning and high-performance team building for managers. One exercise in a week-long training session is to climb a 30-foot pole and leap off the top to catch a trapeze (supported by safety lines, of course). One group included a paraplegic manager in a wheelchair who wanted very much to take part in all the activities. Many in the group had a vapor wall of beliefs and assumptions that said he could not be part of the pole exercise. But he insisted, the trainers huddled, and between them they found a solution. He climbed the pole, using the strength of his arms and the support of safety lines while his team shouted from below. When he reached the top, he cried—and so did we.*
>
> *—Former trainer with SportsMind*

That manager and the trainers who worked with him found a way around the vapor. When the event was over, he said that he would never again feel constrained by the rules.

To Do

★ The next time your employees question you about the rules (about their jobs, the organization, or the work at hand), stop before you say, "It can't be done."

★ Check to see which wall is holding you (and others?) in the box.

★ Unless it is truly the concrete wall, work with your employees to bend or break the rules. Test the vapor wall and the beliefs that box you in. Evaluate new ideas fairly before you discard them.

A manager in a large landscaping company took a look at the rules (mostly vapor) that had him boxed in. His entire team is made up of Gen Ys, and he is a Boomer. He realized that operating by the rules of his generation was hindering his ability to engage and retain younger talent. He decided to let his team do two things that seemed outrageous to him but absolutely normal to them. He said they could paint the office any color (or colors) they wanted, and they could listen to their iPods while they worked. The team was ecstatic. They painted the office in modern, bright colors, happily donned their iPods, and went to work! Productivity and commitment soared. The manager is thrilled he reconsidered the "rules."

Question Yourself, Too

Not only do you need to be able to ask good questions of others, but the best managers we know also are able to ask good questions of themselves. They are able to step back and question actions they have taken and even consider actions they haven't taken. Their continual self-examination catches on with their employees. Here are some questions you might try, adapted with permission from Marilee Adams's book *Change Your Questions, Change Your Life:*[39]

- What happened?

- What's useful about this?

- What do I want?

- What can I learn?

- What is the other person thinking, feeling, needing, and wanting?

- How can this be a win-win?

- What's possible?

- What are my choices?

- What is best to do now?

Bottom Line

How long has it been since you questioned the rules? And how much do you encourage questioning? Allow your employees to ask about the way work gets done and about the rules that hinder their productivity and satisfaction. Support their questioning, and bend or break the rules to help them get what they need. You will greatly increase the odds of keeping your talent.

EIGHTEEN

PROVIDE RECOGNITION

Ponder this: Which matters more, praise or pay?

So this is the chapter about money, right? If not, where is that chapter? Isn't money a major motivator and a key reason people stay in their jobs?

Our competitors all pay 10 to 20 percent more for identical work. They come after us year after year, trying to steal us away from our organization. A few of us have been enticed away. While I would definitely appreciate a raise, I would not leave just to get one. The reason is that I feel rewarded in many other, less tangible ways. I'm rewarded by the actual work I do and by the appreciation my boss always shows. He has told me many times how critical I am to the success of the team. He is caring and finds creative ways to recognize our efforts. I feel important and valued.

—Supervisor, German auto design company

Decades of research and common sense tell you to pay fairly or your best people might leave. Benchmark similar organizations in your industry, and find out what the pay scales, bonuses, and perks look like. If you find that your compensation system is not competitive with that of similar companies, be concerned. Take your findings to your boss or to the compensation expert in your company, and try to get things changed.

Pay fairly and *pay competitively. But don't stop there.* The research that suggests you need to pay fairly to keep your people also says that money alone won't keep them on your team. Money is not the major motivator. Challenge, growth opportunities, flexibility, great coworkers, meaningful work, a good boss, and recognition (often in nonmonetary forms) are examples of things that matter more to most of your people. When those are missing, talented people walk.

Multiple studies around the globe tell us that a majority of people leave their jobs because they don't feel appreciated. What about your employees? Ask them how they are recognized and appreciated. If they immediately respond with "You notice my contributions" or "You thank me all the time," then you're doing great. If they stare blankly at you and then finally say, "Do you mean my paycheck?" you might have some work to do in the rewards department. Stay tuned.

A Word About Perks

What exactly is a perk? It's short for perquisite and is also known as a privilege, a gratuity, a bonus, an incentive, a plus, a benefit, a freebie. The question is, Does a perk work to engage and retain talent?

> *At my company you can do your laundry; drop off your dry cleaning; get an oil change, then have your car washed; work out in the gym; attend subsidized exercise classes; get a massage; study Mandarin, Japanese, and French; and ask a concierge to arrange dinner reservations. How about in your company?*
> —*Research and development manager, Silicon Valley company*

In the last 20 years, we've seen the proliferation of perks in the workplace. Employers have tried everything from volleyball courts to BMW giveaways to concierge services in an attempt to improve work life and to retain talent. While they may have worked to recruit some people, and they are often received happily by the workforce, no evidence exists that perks will help you hang on to your stars. It makes sense that if your highly marketable employees are bored, don't like the boss, or see no career future with you, a massage on Friday afternoons won't keep them!

In this chapter, we'll focus on rewards that really work and are within your control.

Reward Rules

Rule #1: *If an employee expects it, it may no longer be viewed as a reward.*

Alas

Every year I received a bonus, some stock options, and a raise. I was hitting all the targets and doing a good job. It's funny how I left every one of those annual reviews feeling empty. The reward I wanted most was positive feedback from my boss. I wanted him to say that he really appreciated me and my contributions to the business. I really never felt recognized. That was a primary reason I left the company for another job.

—Manager, global automobile manufacturer

You may think that the annual incentive bonus is ample reward for work well done. Your employee may see it differently. Many employees now expect bonuses, company cars, cell phones, financial planning services, and great health care plans as part of the package. Those are no longer useful as special reward or recognition tools.

Rule #2: *Rewards need to match your employees' needs and wants.* How would you like to be recognized? We asked dozens of people this question. The following list represents some of what we heard. Notice the differences.

To Do

Check which forms of recognition you might appreciate. Also note which ones might not matter to you. All of these are requests employees have made to their managers.

★ An award, preferably given in front of my peers

★ A plaque to hang on my wall

★ A thank-you, in writing, from my boss

★ A note to my boss's boss about my excellent performance

★ Frequent pats on the back

★ My boss actually implementing one of my ideas

★ A chance to be on a really exciting, cutting-edge project

★ A day off

★ Words of praise in front of my family

★ A chance to go to lunch with senior management

★ An opportunity to work with people from other parts of the company

★ A chance to be on one of the important steering committees

★ A change in my title

★ Some flexibility in my schedule

★ More freedom or autonomy

★ A seminar or training class

Many managers wrongly assume that everyone likes or wants the same types of rewards and recognition.

I will never forget the thrill of receiving an Excellence Award at the annual company conference. Seven hundred of my peers were there. My name was called and written in huge letters across a massive screen. As I walked forward, it truly felt like an Academy Award moment—almost surreal. There was a cash prize that accompanied a beautiful glass trophy with my name inscribed on it. I had my picture taken with senior management.

The cash was spent within weeks. But the trophy still sits on my desk, and the memory of that amazing moment of recognition will last a lifetime. I have never felt more appreciated or rewarded.

—Vice president, major consulting firm

While this person felt fully rewarded by being in the spotlight at the conference, someone else might have been embarrassed or might have much preferred some other form of recognition. An audience participant in Asia said that in her culture, "The nail that sticks out gets hammered down. It's often awkward for individuals to receive recognition for their excellence. They view it as just doing their duty."

Ask your employees what kind of recognition or reward they most appreciate. Note: In some cultures and some companies, the answer to that question could be "Whatever you want to give is fine." Be patient. Ask "what else?" a few more times and you'll learn just what you need to know about how to reward your treasured employee.

GO TO
―――
Ask
page 1

Thank you
Xie xie
DANKE
Khawp Khun
YUM BONG
Mahalo
Salamat
OBRIGADO
Spacibo
Juspajarana
Arigato
Gracias

Don't you just love those words? Think about how you felt the last time someone thanked you. If it feels so good to receive it, why would we so often fail to give it?

> *So many otherwise able managers act as if compliments come out of their bank accounts.*
>
> —*Warren Bennis, author/consultant*

A study of more than 4,000 businesses across Australia and New Zealand found that three-fourths of employees are starved for recognition, receiving it from their managers only monthly, quarterly, or once a year. And 11 percent received no praise at all.[40] Hope that's not true for you—or for those who report to you!

Check your files. Somewhere in there is a letter from a boss thanking you for a job well done, right? You've cleaned out all the others over the years, but this letter of praise remains. Why is that? Praise works for everyone. There's really no such thing as too much praise (as long as it's sincere). Regardless of individual differences, virtually all employees want to hear how valuable they are to the team, how important their work is, and what great work they have done. And they are happy to hear it again and again.

Compensation is a right; recognition is a gift.

—*Rosabeth Moss Kanter, professor, Harvard Business School*

We suggest you take your employees' individual preferences into account and then do the following:

To Do

Praise your employees in the following ways:

★ *Spontaneously.* Catch people doing something right and thank them then and there. (Thank you, Ken Blanchard, author, *One Minute Manager.*) Leave voice or e-mail recognition messages. And that takes less than one minute.

★ *Specifically.* Praise people for specific (rather than generic) accomplishments or efforts. See "Sentence Starters for Engaging Your Best Employees," coming up.

★ *Purposefully.* Take an employee to lunch or dinner at a great restaurant to show your appreciation of work well done.

★ *Privately.* Go to your employee's office to give a personal thank-you and praise. (*Verbal* thank-yous are critical.)

★ *Publicly.* Praise an employee in the presence of others (peers, family members, your boss). One team adds "shameless bragging" as a short agenda item in all staff meetings.

★ *In writing.* Send a card, letter, memo, or e-mail. Possibly send a copy to team members or higher-level management. Don't forget—*written* thank-yous are a coveted workplace incentive.

A nurse had worked at her hospital for five years. She felt that she was a hard worker and gave more than the job required. However, she had not received much positive feedback along the way from her supervisor. Recently she got a thank-you note in the mail from her manager. The manager told her how much she appreciated her hard work and extra efforts. The participant said that card meant so much to her that she is now carrying it around in her purse (maybe taking a peek at it once in a while). Furthermore, the participant said the thank-you—knowing that the manager appreciates her efforts—"makes all the hard work worthwhile."

Sentence Starters for Engaging Your Best Employees

The HR team at a major bank sent out a memo with recommendations to help managers make their praise more specific. They suggested that telling people "You're doing a great job" isn't going to make them want to stay. Praise can help you retain your top employees—but only if it is detailed and relevant. Here are the "openers" they recommended. Try using any of them with your own employees:

- *"You really made a difference by . . ."*
- *"I'm impressed with . . ."*
- *"You got my attention with . . ."*
- *"You're doing top quality work on . . ."*
- *"You're right on the mark with . . ."*
- *"One of the things I enjoy most about you is . . ."*
- *"You can be proud of yourself for . . ."*
- *"We couldn't have done it without your . . ."*
- *"What an effective way to . . ."*
- *"You've made my day because of . . ."*

Get Creative

As you struggle to think of other ways to reward and recognize your employees, try this. Think about yourself. What could your boss do that would really demonstrate how much he or she values you (besides giving you a raise or praise)? Remembering individual differences, you can use your own list to think about how to reward your employees. Here are a few hints that will get you started.

Time

What a precious commodity. Give an outstanding employee the afternoon off. Allow another to sleep late. Thank a whole team by giving them a day off. Let them decide when to use their gift of time.

One boss created a days-off bank. He put 25 days in the bank and then used those days to reward individuals and teams for outstanding performance.

Toys

What toys might they want? A cappuccino machine? A dart board in the lounge? A volleyball court between buildings? Tickets to the movies?

Alan was so proud. He completed a set of last-minute specifications, stayed late, and in general went above and beyond. To thank him, his boss gave him a $150 check and told him to spend it on a "toy." Alan bought one of those miniature air-ball tables and proudly brought it home. His kids were excited, and when they asked why the gift, he answered, "It's not a gift for you. It's for me, from my company, for doing a great job." The kids were impressed. Four years later the toy is still in use in the family room. When anyone says to his kids, "How cool," they say, "Our dad got it for his good work." Alan smiles every time.

Trophies and Trinkets

What small memento or trophy would be meaningful? It could be a customized plaque, a coffee cup inscribed with a personal thank-you note, or a refrigerator magnet with the perfect message. Often these forms of recognition bring bragging rights and give people a chance to say, "I was recognized because . . . ," and that very public opportunity means a great deal to some people.

Simple observation suggests that most of us are trinket freaks—if they represent a genuine thanks for a genuine assist.

—Tom Peters, author and management consultant

Fun

Would your employees like to take an outing on company time? Leave work early to play ball or to take a hike together? Go to a movie? Have a spontaneous pizza party in the office some afternoon?

GO TO

Kicks
page 98

The team had been working long hours and even weekends. The boss suggested that we rent a limousine, buy some great food and wine, and go to an outdoor concert. He picked up the tab. We felt so pampered and rewarded for all the effort and our outstanding results.

—Vice president, compensation firm

Freedom

What kind of freedom might they want? Flextime? Freedom to work from home, to dress casually, to change the way they do some of the work? Freedom to work without supervision? Freedom to manage a budget?

GO TO

Space
page 183

One manager rewarded his executive assistant by giving her a monthly budget of $400 to use as she saw fit. She could use her judgment to buy anything she thought the team needed. It showed that her boss appreciated and trusted her.

Food

Some of the most popular low-cost rewards are food. One manager we know asks all new hires what their favorite candy is and then delivers that candy to them on their six-month anniversary. (Bev loves Chuckles; Sharon loves peanut M&Ms.) And people love gift certificates for dinner at a great restaurant. (Dinner for two is wonderful—dinner for the family is fantastic!) Use your imagination and find out what your team would really enjoy.

Colleague-to-Colleague Recognition

Have you ever received recognition from a colleague? How did it feel?

> *The Gumby award became treasured. It all started when one employee showed phenomenal flexibility in helping teammates deliver a project on time. He showed up at work the next day to find a giant Gumby doll sitting in his chair. It probably cost $5, but that trophy became the most sought-after prize in the organization, and people were elated when teammates slipped it into their offices.*
>
> *—Consultant, transition consulting firm*

Encourage your talented people to notice their colleagues' contributions, large and small, and to thank them for it. It will catch on and soon you'll have a culture steeped in recognition. The manager of a Gen Y work team encouraged they tweet each other feedback after terrific presentations or new accounts won.

Small Money

Sometimes it's a small sum ($50–$100) to put toward whatever the rewarded employee wants. This discretionary, on-the-spot cash award is sometimes more deeply appreciated than you might ever guess.

> *One internal marketing group in a medium-sized manufacturing company decided to reward people they worked with each month. They set aside*

$1,200 so that they could present a $100 gift certificate to a person in the organization (from any other department) who had worked with them, had helped them in some way, and was appreciated. The entire marketing team selected the recipient, and each month one person surprised the recipient by presenting the gift at a most unexpected time. Everyone loved the idea. The marketing department enjoyed the process, and it was "small money."

Another manager gave everyone on his team two $50 bills three weeks before Christmas. He asked them to give it to someone who needed it. When they shared the stories of how that gift was used, the return on his investment hit the roof.

Big Money

Money might help you get talent in your door, but it will seldom keep them. Yet it may be exactly what some people want. Find out which of your talented employees is truly motivated by money. See what you can do for them. Would a bonus for exceeding goals and expectations help? How about a larger raise than expected? Think about where you can stretch your budget to reward with money when it is warranted and *desired*. Remember, it will usually cost you more to replace stars than to meet their salary requests.

If you think your hands are tied because more dollars aren't available, try this: Tell the truth. Then ask what else your employee might want. At first this may be uncomfortable for both of you. If you are patient, however, other alternatives will appear. You will discover at least one thing your talented employee wants that you can give. The key is that you let employees know how much you value them and their contributions.

Rule of thumb: Compete on culture, not on money. There will always be a higher bidder. Make your workplace so desirable that your talent cannot be enticed away by dollars.

To Do

Since the first edition of *Love 'Em or Lose 'Em*, dozens of managers have sent us their "creative reward" ideas. Here are just a few. Check those you might want to try with your talented people—and add to the list:

★ *The Golden Genie*—I got these great wind-up toys from McDonald's—little genies that walk around. When someone deserves a pat on the back, I put the genie on their desk and let it walk around. Then I grant them any nonmonetary wish they have. I'm amazed; so far there has been nothing I have been unable to grant.

★ *Personalize the Paychecks*—I have a small unit reporting to me. I write a personal note every two-week period, and it goes with their paychecks. Every two weeks, it forces me to think about something I noticed and appreciated. I've gotten great feedback on that.

★ *The Silver Snoopy*—Johnson Space Center (NASA) gives 20 silver Snoopy pins out to employees who have made a big difference to the organization. The silver Snoopy has actually flown in space, so it is a highly valued gift.

★ *A Great Idea*—I give out a light bulb filled with candy to anyone who comes up with a great idea and brings it to me. I generate excitement that says "keep those ideas coming." I give several a month. People actually try to save the candy because they like leaving the light bulb on their desks.

★ *Be the Best*—Once a quarter I ask my team to submit someone else's accomplishment that impressed them. I read over all the accomplishments and give a day off to the award winner. It gives me a chance to see accomplishments I never even knew about, and it gives everyone a chance to recognize their teammates.

★ *Wall of Fame*—I work in a customer service center, and I maintain our "wall of fame." Every time any of my people gets a letter from a customer about their service, it gets framed and put up on the wall. I also give the employee a small gift certificate. I think, though, that their "framed" letter means more than the gift certificate. Visitors love to read the letters. It does great for our internal PR as well.

★ ***Out of the Chair***—I try to remember that people—good, intelligent, capable people—may actually need day-to-day praise and thanks for the job they do. I try to remember to get up out of my chair, turn off my computer, go sit or stand next to them, and see what they're doing. I ask about the challenges, find out if they need additional help, and offer that help when possible. Most of all, I tell them in all honesty that what they are doing is important, to me, to the company, and to our customers.

People are the only asset an organization has that can appreciate over time . . . if we truly appreciate them.

—Anonymous

Culture-Conscious Rewarding

As with every chapter in this book, we've focused again on learning about your talented employees' preferences in order to best engage and retain them. Depending on the size and function of your organization, you might also need to identify recognition preferences on a much larger (even global) scale.

One of my clients recently announced the restructuring of their global rewards program. In the past, when they've given a $100 reward (US dollars) for a certain level of achievement in the US, they've simply converted the dollars into Chinese currency for a Chinese employee who achieved at a comparable level. But the equivalent of $100 US is a much bigger reward in China! So now they're evening out the value of their rewards around the world to make the program more fair.

—Communications consultant in Los Angeles

Is your organization growing? Becoming more multinational or multicultural? If so, you might need to modify your recognition strategies to accommodate the growing diversity. For example, in Australia and Mexico, team recognition seems to be important, according to an OC Tanner study; while in Germany, China, India, and Japan, many employees prefer individual recognition. You'll do well to learn about these and other cultural preferences as you design a recognition system with a *long* reach.

Think about how you will do the following:

- Recognize both global similarities and local nuances.

- Keep your recognition efforts fair and consistent across organizational boundaries, functions, and cultures.

- Adapt recognition methods to the local and cultural preferences of employees.

- Model and encourage global salutes to teammates abroad who do great work.

- Remember to *ask* all employees what kinds of rewards they most value.

Bottom Line

Over and over, research tells us that money is not the major key to engaging and keeping good people. We double-checked this research with our own, and it proves true. When employees across the globe answer the question "What keeps you?" few have dollars in their top three reasons. People want recognition for work well done. Assess your pay scale to be sure it's fair. Then *praise your good people.* Find creative ways to show your appreciation, and you will increase the odds of keeping them.

NINETEEN

GIVE IT

Ponder this: Are your employees on a short leash?

—NOTE—

**If you're wondering how to hold on to your younger workers,
read this chapter!**

Anyone who has raised a teenager (or remembers being one) knows the phrase "Give me some space!" People who feel fenced in, overcontrolled, or frustrated by their lack of power over their own situation usually say it. Dilbert, the cartoon spokesperson for office workers, constantly profiles managers as control freaks who give their employees little or no space, either physically (cubicles) or figuratively (space to control one's own day-to-day existence).

Think about the last boss you had who dictated your every move, held stringently to the policy manual, or was never open to new ways of doing anything. How long did you stay in that job? (We hope you are not there now!) That boss didn't understand inner space or outer space. Employees will leave if they don't have enough of both.

What Are Inner and Outer Space?

By *inner space,* we mean the mental and emotional space your employees want and need to feel like creative, productive members of the team. It includes space to

- be self-directed,

- manage their own time, and

- work and think in new ways.

As a manager, you can give your talented employees the inner space they want and increase the odds that they will stay on your team. (It usually costs you nothing.)

Outer space refers to the physical world and primarily to employees' work environment. It includes space to

- design their own work area,

- work from different places,

- take a break, and

- dress as they wish.

GO TO

Question
page 157

Managing your employees' outer space requests might require some boundary-pushing behaviors for you, especially if your organization has never done it that way. Before we tell you what some other managers are doing to give more space, take this short quiz to determine your own space-giving tendencies. Keep score.

To Do

Read these scenarios, imagining that you're this team's boss. When would you say, "Sure," "No way," or "Let me see what I can do"? Use the answer box that follows.

1. For personal reasons, I want to come in half an hour earlier and leave half an hour earlier three days a week.

2. I want to get this task done in a brand-new way, not as you have seen it done before.

3. I want to complete the first five steps of this project before you review it.

4. I want to try a novel and new approach to increase sales.

5. Instead of taking that class you recommended, I found a mentor to teach me that skill.

6. I just took some great pictures on my vacation and want to put them on my office/cubicle walls.

7. I want to work from home two days a week.

8. I plan to work on Saturdays for a few weeks to finish a project on time. I want to bring my well-trained dog to work with me on those days.

9. I want to wear casual clothes to work, rather than a business suit. I am much more comfortable and creative in my jeans and tennis shoes.

10. I know we've always done these projects solo, but I want to put together a team this time because I believe we will do the job better and more quickly.

11. I want six weeks off work (without pay) to begin building my own home (or: travel, study, care for my parent).

12. I want to bring my baby to work occasionally.

Answer Box

Your Response	1	2	3	4	5	6	7	8	9	10	11	12
Sure, no problem.												
No way.												
Let me see what we can do.												

The list of requests you just considered will give you a clue about the kind of space giving we are talking about. The first five have more to do with inner space, and the remaining seven relate to outer space.

1. Count the number of scenarios where you said, "Sure, no problem, as long as you get the job done."

2. Now count the number where you said, "No way," "It's never been done that way," or "Our policy manual forbids that."

3. Finally, count the number of times you said, "Let me see what we can do," "I will need to take this to my boss," or "Tell me more about what you need, and let's talk about ways it could work."

How Did You Score?

"Sure, no problem."	8 or more	You are *space-friendly*. Keep doing what works!
"No way."	3 or more	You are *space-unfriendly*. Try the "Let's see" response next time!
"Let's see what we can do."	Any number	You are *space-aware*. Your employees will appreciate your efforts!

In some organizations, every one of these requests would receive a positive response. But the opposite is true in far too many. Would you be surprised to know that those organizations are not on anyone's preferred employer list and that they are having greater difficulty recruiting and retaining their employees? We believe that no matter how well these organizations pay, they will ultimately lose their talented people, simply because they do not give them *space!*

So how can you give employees the space they need?

Give Outer Space

Space to Work from Different Places at Different Times

President Barack Obama, speaking at a workplace forum, said, "Work is what you do, not where you are." How do you feel about that? Does your organization support flexible work arrangements? Do you?

In some parts of the globe, flexibility is becoming the norm. The "right to request flexible working" law in Great Britain was enacted in 2002 and extended in 2012 because of its success. "With 96% of employers providing flexible work arrangements to at least some employees, 7 out of 10 employers report flexible work supports employee retention, motivation and engagement. Almost two-thirds of employers believe flexible work supports their recruitment activities and one-half believe it has a positive impact on reducing absence as well as on boosting productivity."[41]

A Eurofound survey reports that remote working (telecommuting) is an option open to 93 percent of employees in Netherlands, 43 percent in Romania, 51 percent in Sweden, and 24 percent in the UK and Italy.[42] And the Telework Research Network (United States, Canada, UK) found that the number of employees working virtually grew by 61 percent from 2005 to 2009, and it is estimated to grow to 69 percent by 2016. Seventy-nine percent of survey respondents said they prefer to work virtually, and 61 percent would take a pay cut to do so.[43]

Many managers who've tried it say that telecommuters tend to work longer hours because they feel telecommuting is a privilege and they want to make sure they don't lose it. Productivity and morale go up, while turnover and real estate costs go down.

Job performance of employees working at least partially from home is clearly increased. Employees working in company offices are interrupted from their work on average, every 11 minutes—and then need 8 minutes to regain full concentration.

—Hartmut Schutze, professor, University of Applied Sciences and Arts, Switzerland

But what if your organization does not allow flexible work arrangements?

My company had never allowed telecommuting, and I believed it probably never would. One of my top employees asked me if she could work from home two days a week, and my immediate response was no. A month later she sadly handed in her resignation and said she had found an employer who would allow her to telecommute. I simply could not afford to lose her, so I went to my boss and asked if we might bend the rules on a trial basis, offer her telecommuting two days a week, and see how productive she was. She stayed with us, increased her actual productivity by 10 percent, and is a grateful, loyal employee. Since then we have loosened our policy substantially and consider telecommuting on a case-by-case basis for any employee who requests it.

—Accounting manager, city government in Switzerland

This manager not only bent the rules (probably after reading the Q chapter) but also realized the importance of space.

Telecommuting is not an option for jobs that simply must be performed at the work site. (Consider a nurse on duty, the landscaper at your home, the factory worker on the line.) If the work site is the only place an employee can perform that job, think about other ways that you can give your employees space.

Sometimes the organization has no rule about working from another place, but the manager says no anyway. If you are one of those managers, ask yourself why. Is it a lack of trust in your employees? Is it concern that they will "goof off" or not be productive without your ever-vigilant eye? If so, consider managing based on results. Be clear about your expectations: what do you want them to produce or create? By when? Consider letting your employees get those results from whatever location they wish.

Alas

I think of myself as cutting-edge in many ways. But in other ways I think I'm stuck in old paradigms and bound by old rules. I've lost three key employees in the past year. Each one wanted something I couldn't (or thought I couldn't) give—like a chance to telecommute two days a week or dress casually. Recently I saw another manager work out a deal with one of her prized employees. She got permission for him to work very different hours from everyone else. He's thrilled and producing like crazy. Now I'm rethinking my tendency to say no immediately to requests coming my way. Maybe I need to be more flexible in order to keep the talent on my team.

—Manager, global hotel chain

Give Space to Take a Break

A talented young engineer in a large aerospace firm asked his immediate boss for six weeks off work (without pay) to begin building his house. His boss said okay, even though the engineer's absence would certainly be a hardship. After the six weeks, the engineer asked for an additional four weeks, as he just hadn't done as much as he had hoped on his house. The boss pondered the request, thought about how valued this employee was, ran the request up to the division engineer, and came back with the okay. The engineer remained a loyal, committed employee for another 24 years. He later became a member of the senior management team and helped lead his company to tremendous success. When asked what he would have done had they turned down his request, he said he would have quit the job and found a new one after completing his project.

Seldom do we find managers who value their employees enough to allow them the space to take a real break from work. Yet in many countries and in certain fields (such as college teaching), sabbaticals are actually encouraged. Employers support valuable employees in their decisions to travel, learn something new, or simply go to the mountains and meditate. The next time your talented employee asks you for a break, get creative (with the employee) about finding a way to make it happen. Your employee will feel supported, and the odds of your retaining that talent will go up.

Me: *Where are you going?*

Seatmate: *I'm taking a leave of absence. My wife and I are traveling to New Zealand, Australia, and Indonesia. We'll be gone for two months.*

Me: *Wow. Who do you work for?*

Seatmate: *Boeing.*

Me: *Hmm. Is Boeing pretty good about that kind of thing? Giving that kind of flexibility?*

Seatmate: *It's all about your individual manager. My manager says, "If you can swing it, you can do it."*

Give Space to Dress How One Wishes

We have all read about the high-tech environment in which people with creative, brilliant minds dress in all kinds of bizarre outfits. Some wonder if it is appropriate or professional or conducive to productivity. The results seem to speak for themselves. Just take a look at successful companies where there are *no dress codes* in many departments. How productive have they been over the years? Managers in those environments say that their employees often work long hours (sometimes 70-hour weeks) by their own choosing as they strive to complete a project or get a new product out the door. Allowing them to dress as they wish seems a small concession, considering the commitment and high productivity.

I don't feel I need to dress up to meet an equation.

—*Mathematician*

Think about where you can offer flexibility in dress. Is it Friday-casual day? Summer attire? Different dress codes for those who never see a customer? Challenge the rules a bit. Are they reasonable? If business wear is truly necessary, then you will want to support the rule—but think about the requirements realistically and with a creative eye. It is truly amazing how favorably many employees view a flexible dress code.

Give Space to Design One's Space

Should all work areas in your organization look alike? Anyone who has studied personality differences knows that one way we express our uniqueness is in our surroundings. Our homes, our offices, and our cubicles will reflect our style if we have the freedom.

Many organizations today hire interior decorating firms that design beautiful, perfect work areas. In some of those workplaces, the decorating rules are quite explicit, and there is no room for personalization. What about your organization? If the rules allow for some flexibility, then you as a manager have room to allow space for your employees. Let them bring in their favorite pictures and organize their desks the way they wish. Do not demand that everyone have work spaces like yours.

Workers' cubicles could be their castles—with a little help. One manager gave his employees a small decorating stipend for personalizing their workplaces. They were thrilled and have done some very creative things to make their cubes their castles. With a little bigger budget, workers have opted for changes like these to their workspaces:

- Cubicle walls that hold oxygen-giving plant life, complete with built-in irrigation

- Adjustable desks to accommodate the shorter or taller employee

- Shorter walls and privacy shields to allow for more or less interaction

- Noise canceling speakers to facilitate concentration
- Fold-out chairs to welcome guests to a small space

Giving Inner Space

Give Space to Be Self-Directed—to Work and Think in Their Own Unique Ways

Giving inner space requires that managers *let go and trust* their talented employees to manage and continuously improve their work.

> *Leaders at a large retail store know a lot about giving employees space and empowering them to make decisions and manage their own work. In fact, managers credit their corporate culture for one of the highest retention rates in the retail industry. The primary rule, stated in the employee handbook, is this: use your good judgment at all times.*

Space-friendly managers have

- pushed for nap rooms for employees who need a midmorning or afternoon snooze to reenergize;
- said "sure" to their younger employees who wanted to work while listening to their iPods;
- allowed an employee to work on his laptop on the lawn (where he could think!);
- agreed to a webinar instead of a classroom;
- purchased a standing desk for an employee who asked.

To Do

★ Let your employees manage more aspects of their own work, without direct supervision.

★ Trust them to get it right and then assist when they need your help.

★ Allow them to try new ways of accomplishing their tasks, even if "it's never been done that way before."

You probably have plenty of leeway as a manager to give *inner space* to your employees, and the payoff is tremendous. If you cannot offer telecommuting or casual dress codes, you *can* offer the power to manage the way they do the day-to-day work.

Give Space to Manage One's Own Time

All the research points to the fact that emerging workers (of any age) want flexibility in work schedules.

So what are organizations doing in response to these wants?

A large medical center found the job market for medical professionals like nurses and pharmacists, was, in part, driving flexible scheduling. Offering schedules to fit various lifestyles and needs made the organization more competitive. For example, one emergency room nurse chose to work a "power weekend," which has her on duty for 12 hours on Saturday and Sunday, with time off during the week to pick up grandchildren at school and attend their sporting events.

—*Director, Human Resources*

What if yours isn't one of these flex-friendly employers? This may be another area where you say, "I have no control. Our organization has strict policies about work hours and how and where they are spent." If that is true, then you will want to consider other ways of offering space to your employees. However, we encourage you to see where there *might* be some flexibility to offer your employees space to manage their work time according to their own unique needs.

One supervisor we know allowed workers to arrive 10 minutes before their shifts began and leave 10 minutes earlier or vice versa. He realized that this 10-minute window could substantially reduce driving time during rush hours, making a huge difference in his employees' stress.

Oh, and consider the "B-Society," a group in Denmark lobbying for businesses to be flexible and accommodate people who just can't get going before 10 or 11 in the morning.[44] Accommodating the B-Society late-sleepers is gaining popularity—worldwide. Can you find a way to harness the energy of your talent when they're at their best?

What About Fairness?

Our readers have asked us about fairness. "How do I give one employee time off on Friday afternoon and not give it to everyone?" Being fair does not mean treating everyone identically.

Do you have more than one child? If so, do you give them all identical holiday gifts? Probably not.

The answer is mass customization (sounds like an oxymoron, doesn't it?), and it offers a new kind of institutional fairness. The workforce is more differentiated, and one policy simply does not fit all. (Who said management was easy?) Listen to your talented employees' requests, and brainstorm with them to create innovative solutions that are *fair,* both to them and to their talented teammates—the ones you also want to keep!

> *Of course, there's a catch. Sure, you can take Friday off to train for the Iron-man Triathlon or to attend your kid's soccer match. Just make sure you do your job—and figure out how to do it better than anyone else. With freedom and flexibility come responsibility and accountability—lots of it.*
>
> *—Paula Lawlor, MediHealth Outsourcing*

Bottom Line

Allowing job sharing, flextime, telecommuting, or working on the lawn on a laptop are not pampering. They are ways to meet your business goals. That means listening to what people want, going to bat for their needs, and ultimately giving them options and opportunities to do things differently. Truly listen to the unique requests your employees bring you. Ask them to provide ideas for how this change might work—for you, the team, the organization. Make an honest attempt to win flexibility and improved work conditions for your people.

Enjoy space to play, have a good time, take breaks, celebrate successes, creatively attack problems—all of this makes for an engaged, productive workforce. Your reward will be loyalty and commitment from your best people.

TWENTY

Truth

TELL IT

Ponder this: How often are you giving and getting feedback?

Are you an honest person? Do you believe in telling the truth? Most people will answer yes to both questions.

Our studies show that employees yearn for straight talk. They want to *hear* the truth about their performance and the organization. They want to *tell you* the truth about your performance. When the truth is missing, people may feel demoralized, less confident, and ultimately less loyal. Of course you know where that might lead—right out your door and through the competition's. Tell the truth if you want to engage and keep your good people.

A New View of Truth Telling

The secret of truth telling is to view it as a *gift*. If you believe that giving truthful, balanced feedback to people will help them to be more effective in their careers and perhaps in life, then you will be more inclined to give that feedback.

Have you ever taken music, dance, or karate lessons or had a soccer, rugby, or golf coach? Think back to that time and recall one of your lessons.

Did he demonstrate a better way to grip the club? Did she help you develop better rhythm? Weren't they constantly helping you fine-tune your approach? The feedback was probably balanced between *praise*—"That was great. Play it again just like that!"—and *correction*—"This time kick the ball more like this." Their gift was honest feedback, from someone willing to tell you there was still room for improvement and committed to helping you get there.

Your employees expect and need the same kind of coaching from you today.

Are they getting it? Perhaps not. Gallup's ongoing, global, Q12 engagement research (47,000 respondents in 116 countries) gives us a clue. At the bottom of the ranking is the item that asks employees whether someone at work has talked to them about their progress in the last six months. This finding suggests that managers are not providing workers with regular, individualized, truthful feedback.[45]

Tell Them the Truth About Their Work

Think about the people who work with you or report to you. Consider their relative strengths and weaknesses, their blind spots, their overused strengths, and the flaws that may stall them. Have you been honest and direct about your perceptions with these people?

I wish I could have a dollar for the number of occasions I've had to untangle a situation where at the outset if there had been a clear, thoughtful expression of truth, there would be no mess!

—Matt Hawkins, Leadership Development,
Tandem Ministries, New Zealand

When and how did you give them your input? Even the best bosses might honestly confess that they have trouble giving people direct feedback, especially about possible flaws or areas where employees need improvement. Most of us were not trained to give negative news. Our elders taught us that "honesty is the best policy," but we also learned, "If you can't say something nice, don't say anything at all." So we don't.

Managers say they hesitate to give critical feedback because they

- are afraid of hurting feelings or demoralizing employees—even prompting them to quit.

- are concerned about appearing arrogant or abrasive.

- are uncomfortable giving bad news or find it easier to give only positive news.

- are not sure they're 100 percent right.

- worry about a defensive reaction.

- work in a polite organization where critical feedback isn't given.

- don't like to judge other people.

When I give feedback, I'm signaling to people that I'm interested in their future.

—Larry Bossidy, coauthor, Execution:
The Discipline of Getting Things Done

Alas

I honestly thought I was doing a great job. I had been promoted several times, had had positive performance reviews, and had received a bonus every year. The next thing I knew, I was passed over for a big promotion, shoved in a corner, and ignored. When the downsizing happened, I was laid off. Only then did I hear that there had been some problems with my management style through the years.

—Unemployed middle manager

Ask Them for Their View

Neuroscientists tell us that beginning with a question will reduce fear. If you are one of those managers who finds giving feedback difficult, consider asking your employees to provide their own points of view first. What is their view of the past quarter? What areas of their performance do they feel best about? What successes have they had? Probe for the specific skills they used.

Ask, too, what they might do to be even more effective. Where do they most need to grow? Ask them about a recent project that they might do differently if they had the chance. Ask what they learned from the experience. Most employees know the answers to these questions, especially if they're fortunate enough to have had truth-telling managers.

The Truth Hurts—or Does It?

When employees in most organizations are asked what they would like more of from their managers, their first response is usually *feedback*. People want to know where they stand—they want to know if your perception of their performance is the same as their own.

Years of research (much of it done by the Center for Creative Leadership) confirms that the absence of honest feedback derails leaders at all levels.

Sometimes that means people lose their job, but more often it means they fail to fulfill their promise.

Even the high-potentials in your organization need honest, balanced feedback. Too often they hear only how wonderful, bright, and talented they are. Without feedback, these employees can come to a startling, shocking halt after several promotions, big raises, and starring roles. Why? Because no one helped them see their rough edges and the need for continual improvement. They began to believe their own press and developed major blind spots. Their confidence turned into arrogance, in part because of insufficient, inaccurate, imbalanced, or tardy feedback from key people in their lives. The truth could have saved them.

To Do

★ Jot down the names of each of your direct reports. Next to each name write the words "more of," "less of" and "continue." List some behaviors and action steps in each category. What would you like to see them doing differently or continuing to do? And what difference would it make to them, to you, to the team?

★ Gather up your courage and talk to them! Ask for their reaction and their perspective to the feedback you're giving.

"But I Already Gave Feedback—in December"

In many organizations, managers are only required to give feedback during the annual performance review. They give input to reward and reinforce employees' behaviors and performance, to justify the annual raise, or to warn them about unsatisfactory performance and possible consequences. Some managers gloss over the negatives and focus on the good news only, and others do just the opposite. In either case, the reviews don't tell the whole truth, and employees are often left frustrated by the whole process.

Consider these two points:

- Formal performance appraisal meetings are important. If you handle it badly, your employees may feel dismissed and unimportant. Plan carefully and balance the good news (positive) with the important news (room for improvement).

- Don't give feedback just once a year. To retain your key people, it is essential that you give regular, honest input about their work.

Alas

In our organization, the employee and boss both fill out the performance appraisal form once a year. The idea is to compare results and have a discussion about the employee's performance and where he might improve. I spent hours filling mine out, really trying to evaluate my strengths and weaknesses and how I had done in reaching my goals. I turned it in to my boss three weeks before our "big meeting." When I showed up, it became clear that he had not looked at my report at all and had filled in his form in a hurry, just minutes before the meeting. All the ratings were just average, and when I asked him how I could bring them up, he said he would have to think about it. Twenty minutes later he said he had another meeting. So—I had waited all year to get feedback from my boss, and when it finally came, it was mediocre and almost meaningless. I have never felt so insignificant—maybe I need to start looking around for another job.

—Nursing supervisor, hospital

"What If I Don't Know How?"

Many managers are uncomfortable giving feedback (positive or negative) because they don't know how to do it simply and effectively. Many have never had a good role model. Giving feedback so that it doesn't put employees on the defensive is key. How do you measure up? Take this quiz to see if you are feedback-savvy.

Feedback Quiz

My feedback . . .

- is private. (I choose a place where the person can hear my comments without being distracted or embarrassed.) ___ True ___ False

- receives the time it deserves. (I plan the time and use it just for the purpose of giving feedback to someone.) ___ True ___ False

- is frequent. (I give feedback immediately after actions that need to be changed or rewarded.) ___ True ___ False

- focuses more on the future than the past. (I talk mostly about what can be done to improve, rather than what went wrong.) ___ True ___ False

- is specific, with clear examples. ("I think you need to delegate more. You did last quarter's entire project yourself.") ___ True ___ False

- gives information that helps the person to make decisions. ("Your team wants you to involve them more in planning.") ___ True ___ False

- gives suggestions for growth and improvement. ("I think you could work on negotiating skills, especially if you want that new role.") ___ True ___ False

- allows for discussion. ("Tell me what you are thinking. What do you want to do about this?") ___ True ___ False

- creates next steps. ("Let's meet again next week to create a development plan for you. Meanwhile, think about what you'd like to include in that plan.") ___ True ___ False

- preserves dignity (Is given in a caring, face-saving manner) ___ True ___ False

In China we often go through a third party when giving feedback. That's in order for the recipient to save face. It's hard to have plain honest conversation, given the power differential between boss and employee. That's where the trusted third party comes in. Remember to treat each other with honesty and sincerity—坦诚相待

—Consultant in Singapore

How did you do? If most of these statements are true for you, fantastic! Now go ask your employees if they agree. Ask them to tell you the truth.

Confidentially Speaking

Another popular approach is 360-degree feedback: employees receive feedback from you, their peers, mentors, customers, and direct reports. The feedback also includes a self-assessment that lets people compare their own perceptions with the views of others. The 360-degree feedback highlights both strengths and opportunities to improve, and its purpose is developmental. Because it is usually anonymous, raters tend to be very honest. It is valuable for all of us to get input from someone other than the boss; this process is just one way of doing that.

Note: Be sure to follow up with coaching and support for people who get critical feedback about behaviors they need to change. Getting the feedback is usually just the first step; most people will need help creating and implementing a development plan.

Tell Them the Truth About the Organization

Research overwhelmingly supports the notion that engaged employees are "in the know." They want to be trusted with the truth about the business, including its challenges and downturns.

We know, however, that there may be times when you are simply not at liberty to tell the whole truth. A pending merger, reorganization, or change at the top of the organization could be off-limits for discussion with your team.

GO TO

Information
page 77

Managers sometimes hold information back in the belief that it makes them more powerful or that it is better for their employees not to know. When you have bad news, give it face-to-face and as soon as possible. If you make a mistake, confess, tell them the truth, and accept responsibility. Your personal stock will go up, and so will the trust level on your team.

Ask Them for the Truth (Even about You)

We would rather be ruined by praise then saved by criticism.

—*Norman Vincent Peale*

So far we've been talking about telling the truth to your employees. But what about getting them to tell you the truth? Many managers (especially at high levels) have had no formal performance reviews or feedback sessions for years. By the time they rise to the top, they might be getting almost no balanced, accurate input about how they get the work done. Often, leaders are rewarded as long as they hit their bottom-line targets.

Who, then, tells the senior leader about his warts? Probably no one. That absence of truthful, balanced feedback creates leaders who have missed the opportunity to grow, to be even more effective in their jobs, and to keep their talented people.

In a weekly staff meeting, I told my employees I wanted feedback about my skills as a manager. I told them I'd had input that I could be better at delegation and employee development. I asked them to rate me on a 1–10 scale on each of those skills and then to tell me what I would need to do differently to be scored a 10. One person told me I was already a 10—that got a laugh from the group. We agreed they would type their responses and give them to my assistant. She delivered the anonymous responses to me, and I shared them with my group at the next staff meeting. They know what I'm working on and are willing to give me more feedback as I try to improve.

—*Sales VP, global biotech company*

In almost every setting outside the modern organization, experts and masters continue to ask for the truth about their performance, and they strive for improvement. Athletes, musicians, and martial arts masters are examples of how people use honest feedback to refine their skills even more. Imagine what you, as a leader, could learn if your employees felt comfortable speaking up or pushing back. Imagine what that learning could do for you, your team and your organization.

The Corporate Executive Board tracks seven key financial indicators in more than 130 companies worldwide, and "the one most strongly correlated with ten-year returns is employees' comfort in speaking up, even when they have negative things to say."[46] We know one manager who used the jerk checklist (page 90) to get some very interesting feedback! Find a way that works for you—and for the people on your team.

You can establish an environment where truth is welcome. And you can serve as a model for your employees as they watch how you *seek and receive* feedback. View the truth as a gift.

> *Thanks for the feedback. Send socks next time.*
> —*UK sales manager with a good sense of humor*

Bottom Line

Talented people want to hear the truth about themselves and the organization. They need to feel free to tell you the truth as well. Honest feedback is a gift you can both give and receive. Truth telling can help keep your talented people engaged and growing. Tell—and hear—the truth.

TWENTY-ONE

Understand

LISTEN DEEPER

Ponder this: When you tune out, do you miss out?

"You're not listening. You never listen." If you ever hear these complaints, at home or at work, read on.

Why is there no end to the training courses on this subject? Why do feedback surveys repeatedly tell managers that they are lousy listeners? Why don't we *get it*?

Many managers don't really believe that listening is a critical skill. They believe that being results oriented or customer focused is much more important to business success than being a good listener. Are they right?

Ivan understands me. He listens to me—and I feel understood. The more he listens, the more I reveal, and the stronger our relationship becomes. We have developed a huge amount of trust. With other bosses, I used to edit. I tell Ivan everything. As a result, he is never surprised. He has a better handle on things. Because of our bond, we are more creative, take bigger risks, push the boundaries, and accomplish amazing things. I have never had a better boss, and I have never been so productive. Right now, nothing could entice me away from this job.

—*Vice president, global engineering organization*

A common characteristic of all effective love 'em managers is they are great listeners! How are you doing in that regard?

Write down three or four things you learned from your employees this week. It could be process improvement ideas they have, a customer (or family) challenge they face, or a team issue they struggle with. If you can't list three or four things you learned, you probably have not been listening carefully enough to your employees.

Communication is critical to keeping your talent. If they feel heard, understood, and valued by you, they will work harder and produce more. They will want to stay and work for you. And if they don't—they will disengage or depart.

Pay Attention, Please

The manager's head moves up and down. She says, "Uh-huh," 35 times in a row. Is she listening? Probably not. So what gets in the way of listening deeper? What are you thinking about while your employee talks?

To Do

Which of these do you sometimes think while your employees talk to you? Be honest.

- ★   I already know the punch line. I'm five steps ahead.
- ★   I'm too busy for this. I have a stack of work on my desk.
- ★   He's getting emotional. I'm checking out.
- ★   Now what should my response be? How can I defend my position?

★ She's so boring. I'm going to check my e-mail while she talks.

★ That's not relevant.

★ You're so off-target.

★ There's nothing new here.

★ We solved that a long time ago.

How did you do? You might believe that it is great time management (multitasking) to have your mind busy while another person talks or to be planning your response so that you are ready the minute the employee stops speaking. You might be impatient. You might believe that your time and ideas are worth more than your employee's. Or you may have just forgotten how to really focus on a person and listen deeply. Regardless of your reason, the result is the same. *When you tune out, you miss out.* You miss out on information. More important, you miss out on having a respectful relationship.

Learn to listen. You don't learn anything from hearing yourself talk.

—*Leo Buscaglia*

Listening Is a Choice

For most of my career, I was an awful listener in almost every possible way. I was arrogant throughout my 30s, for sure—maybe into my early 40s. My conversations were all about some concept of intellectual winning and "I'm going to prove I'm smarter than you." It wasn't an evil, megalomania-driven thing; it was mostly because I was a striver. I wanted to get ahead, and getting ahead meant convincing people of my point of view. (www.mckinsey quarterly.com/article)

—*Amgen former CEO Kevin Sharer*

Kevin Sharer *chose* to become a better listener. That's the first step to making it happen. Simply choose.

You might already have great listening skills and habits, but you may be selective about when you use them. Be conscious about how you are listening to your employees. Decide to listen deeper. Be curious about the talented people who report to you.

> *What stands out most, and what kept me at that company for many years, was really a simple thing. Every Friday we'd get together at a local pub, and the general manager would come in and start the party with one question, "So, how was your week?" We'd all go on and on about the problems we had faced, the successes we'd had, the issues that we still had to deal with. We didn't really solve much (although that happened occasionally). Mostly we all just vented. And the amazing thing was, he was truly interested. We went home those weekends feeling great.*
>
> *—Employee, furniture retail company*

Sometimes you've got to see the reason for better listening. One executive said that when he worked in Japan, he found a reason and he learned to really listen. The reason was comprehension. He was listening so intently and striving to truly understand what people were trying to convey. He was not listening so that he could critique or object or convince.

Listening to understand helps you get information you need to be effective as a manager. It's a form of field research and gives you crucial signals from your ecosystem. In the process, you're showing respect to the people doing the talking!

Listen Up

Experts have been writing about the importance of listening in the world of work . . . forever! Still, leaders who don't listen remain one of the biggest complaints on the part of employees everywhere. Kenny Moore, in his book *The CEO and the Monk*, suggests that listening has become a lost art in business.

Become a better communicator by keeping your mouth shut. We risk creating a culture where the ones that speak the most and the loudest win out. My instincts tell me that that's not going to satisfy our customers, whether external or internal. There is something to be said for maintaining a quiet demeanor. Silence on our part invites the thoughts and opinions of others, a true recipe for sustained growth and competitive advantage.[47]

★ ★ ★ ★ ★

WAIT!

Why

Am

I

Talking?

—*Al-Anon*

If you notice you're talking more than you're listening, try doing the opposite. It will take practice and patience (and feedback from those around you) to make the change, but you'll find it worth the effort!

Here is one way to get started.

The Blinking Word

Many managers are becoming better listeners by learning a simple technique called the *blinking word*. Here is how it works:

Scenario: Your employee, Shelby, asks to talk to you, so you schedule a meeting in your office. You welcome Shelby in and ask what you can do for her. She says, "I'm having trouble with one of my employees. He seems to lack motivation for the job."

1. Identify the words that blink (stand out). *"I'm having **trouble** with one of my employees. He seems to **lack motivation** for the job."*

2. Ask about one of the blinking words. *"What kind of trouble?"* or *"How does he seem to lack motivation?"*

3. Listen for Shelby's answer. *"He's not as **productive** as he used to be."*

4. Notice the blinking word in her answer and question it. *"How has his productivity dropped?"*

5. Listen for Shelby's answer. *"He gets **less** work done in a week, and the **quality has slipped**, too."*

6. Notice the blinking word in her answer and question it. *"Why do you think he is getting less work done?"* or *"Tell me about the slip in quality."*

7. Keep going, watch for the blinking words, and ask about them.

Use open questions as you follow the blinking words. Open questions begin with words like *how, why, where, when,* and *tell me about.* They are designed to avoid yes or no responses, which often lead to a dead end. As you follow the blinking word, you go deeper into Shelby's problem. Meanwhile, Shelby feels listened to. She believes that you care about her dilemma and are there to help her solve it. The blinking word technique will force you to listen empathetically, at the deepest level. You will not be able to tune in and out and still follow the blinking word. (P.S. *Do* try this at home. Your spouse, kids, and friends will be pleasantly surprised at what a good listener you have become.)

Alas

I watched him read his e-mail while his employees talked to him. I was on the receiving end of that behavior a few times myself. He probably thought we didn't notice or that we respected his ability to multitask. He was wrong. We felt unimportant and unheard most of the time.

—Front-line employee

Listening Liabilities

If you truly want to become a better listener, be honest about whether any of these behaviors prevents you from hearing what your employees have to say.

Interrupting

Do you interrupt with your own ideas so that you stop others midsentence? Your employees will lose patience with you and may quit coming to you with their ideas and challenges if you interrupt them at every turn.

Notice when you interrupt your employees. Use the blinking word technique. Let them do the talking while you do the listening. Let them finish.

Defending

Do you get defensive when others don't agree with your stance on a topic? Do you move quickly to arguing your point of view? Stop defending and let your employees explain their thinking or their position on a topic. Try to really understand them before you rush to your own defense.

Transmitting

Do you transmit more than you receive? What percentage of the time are you typically talking? Twenty percent? Eighty percent? Try giving your employees a chance to say more.

The Greek philosopher Zeno is said to have offered this advice: "The reason we have two ears and only one mouth is that we may hear more and speak less."

Drifting

Does your mind wander during a conversation so that you lose track and have to ask the other person to repeat things? If you use the blinking word technique, you can't help but stay focused.

Derailing

Do you change the subject frequently and steer it to something that interests you more? Get interested, get curious—about them. Find what's fascinating about these talented people and what they have to say. Your interest in them will pay off.

Rambling

Do you wonder, "Why would I use 5 words when I can use 20?" If you're succinct, they'll have more time to talk.

Opinion Giving

Do you offer opinions and advice even when neither is wanted? Ask a few great questions instead and listen to the wisdom emanating from your talented employees.

Putting Down

If you haven't said these things, you've no doubt heard them:

- That's not relevant.
- You've got to be kidding.
- This is all you have?
- That makes no sense.
- You're off target.
- There's nothing new here.
- We solved that a long time ago.
- I can't believe you didn't know that.

How does it feel when you're on the receiving end of these put-downs? Demoralized? Not valued? Disrespected? Notice if—or when—you accidentally deploy one of these weapons. Catch yourself and course-correct. Get curious, ask questions, and LISTEN.

Multitasking

It is impossible to truly listen while you watch TV, read your e-mail, think about dinner, or organize your desk. Some of us remain in a stubborn state of denial about this reality—but that doesn't make it any less real. Google "multitasking pitfalls." The research is voluminous and solid. Bottom line: *stop doing whatever you're doing and listen* to your talented employees. (Try this for a week at home, too, and watch what happens with your relationships!)

Listen Deeper

> *Every person I work with knows something better than I—my job is to listen long enough to find it and use it.*
>
> —Jack Nicklaus, champion golfer

GO TO
———
Reward
page 168

Some managers wonder, "What should I be listening for?" We believe it is important to listen for the following:

- **Input.** Talented people want to have an ear for their great ideas and solutions. They want to be heard and recognized.

  My boss not only listened to my ideas, but she let me present them at the board meeting. I felt so proud.

  —*Manager, real estate management firm*

- **Motivations.** What do they want from this job and from you? What gets them up in the morning and looking forward to their work?

  He asked me what I liked about the job and what I wasn't so thrilled with. He listened. Once he really understood where I was coming from, he suggested that we hand off some of my least favorite tasks to a colleague who likes doing that work. He seems to really understand me.

  —*Supervisor, medical group*

- **Challenges.** You need to know about your employees' obstacles.

One of my direct reports has a talented employee, Denise, whose performance level had dropped. We were wondering why. I suggested that we both meet with her. We asked Denise if something was bothering her, and she began to talk. Finally, she shared that she was battling cancer but had been afraid to tell us. We listened to her for two hours. She said that she felt so much better now that the secret was out, and she thanked us for our support and understanding. That was two years ago. Denise has made it through the tough times and has recently been promoted.

—Director, global advertising firm

Some of our readers have said they are uncomfortable listening deeply, especially about employees' lives outside work. They fear heartfelt conversations may take them to a personal level or an empathetic state that leaves them vulnerable.

Some managers don't want their people to discuss their personal lives at all. I say, bring it on. If people can get something off their chest for an hour, I've got them for the next 20 (or more).

—Team leader, small manufacturing plant

★ ★ ★ ★ ★

I hire knowledge workers. I need their brainpower. If they are unhappy with me, the organization, or their personal lives, they show up at work with half a brain. I can't afford that. I listen to their problems, help them brainstorm solutions, and refer them to helpful resources. I work very hard to keep them happy.

—Executive, German high-tech company

You don't have to play counselor, and you don't have to have answers to their personal problems. Just listen.

Bottom Line

Get to know your people. Make time to understand them by really listening to them. Notice your own listening style and improve it (there's always room). Your efforts will pay off. Employees who feel heard and understood will stay engaged and on your team. Those who don't will find another place to work, with a boss who will listen.

TWENTY-TWO

Values

DEFINE AND ALIGN

Ponder this: What matters most to them?

Values define what we consider to be important. They are the standards for measuring our bottom-line needs. And more than anything, they are the engine for our actions.

> *Values are the emotional salary of work, and some folks are drawing no wages at all.*
>
> —*Howard Figler*

How do your employees' values align with their work? With the organization? With you? How can you find out? And how can you help them realign if necessary?

Values Go to Work

Whether you work in Detroit, Dublin, or Dubai, you take your values with you every day. You don't get to leave them at home. They help you perform and excel. And it's best when they match up with the work you've agreed to do.

Conflicts over values increase the risk of losing employees far more than conflicts over pay. People want to spend time doing something they truly value. When their work and values align, your talent is most likely to stay engaged and on your team. So how will you learn about what your talented people value most? Ask.

Try some of these questions:

- Which parts of your job give you the greatest satisfaction?

- What do you need most from your work? Does the job deliver?

- What makes for a really good day?

- What would you miss if you left this job?

- What did you like best about other jobs you've had?

- What small steps can we take to increase the value proposition for you in this job?

- Tell me about a time when you really felt energized at work.

As they answer, probe for specifics. Does "a good day" mean more customer contact, giving a speech, leading a task force, or helping a new employee get settled on the team?

My work is often physically difficult. I leave work exhausted but with a smile on my face. You see, I get to help over a dozen elderly patients every single day. I help them with the activities of daily living—but I also help them find joy in their day. I make a point to visit, to ask about their families, to read cards and letters they've received. I could make more money and do less strenuous work in another career. But I love helping people. This job is all about helping.

—Nurse aide in the Philippines

If you want to pursue the values question further, try the following exercise at your next staff meeting. Discuss what happens to learn more about how values show up in the world of work.

To Do

Show employees this list of value choices. Listen to their responses and dig deeper where you can.

★ When you go to work, you look forward to

  a. having new challenges.

  b. enjoying the company of coworkers.

  c. planning your own day.

  d. the structure of routine.

★ When you have a new project to work on, you're excited if

  a. you will learn new things.

  b. you will get to work with new people.

  c. you will be in control.

  d. it will be low stress.

★ If you won the lottery, one thing that might keep you from quitting your job would be

  a. the excitement of competition.

  b. missing friends at work.

  c. having work goals to motivate you.

  d. not knowing what to do with your time.

★ In your ideal job, you would

  a. have opportunities to be creative.

  b. help society.

  c. start your own business.

  d. never work more than eight hours a day.

★ Looking back, you felt most satisfied with work when

    a. you were involved in exciting projects.

    b. you interacted with people outside your own department.

    c. you worked totally independently.

    d. work doesn't interfere with home life.

★ You work best when

    a. your curiosity and energy are high.

    b. you're working with a team.

    c. you're working primarily alone.

    d. there are no deadlines.

★ Success, to you, means

    a. always pursuing excellence.

    b. working closely with friends.

    c. being the master of your own future.

    d. being content with your work.

A Quick Guide That Might Guide You

"A" answers suggest that these people are goal oriented. Help them find opportunities to work on stimulating projects that lead to clear-cut results and a sense of accomplishment.

"B" answers suggest that these employees are people oriented. Look for ways to increase their interpersonal contacts at work, perhaps through participation on task forces and project teams.

"C" answers indicate self-starters. Find situations that reward self-motivation with even more freedom and independence. Don't micromanage these people.

"D" answers suggest that these people seek balance and an orderly work routine. Good soldiers, these people will need the greatest attention and re-assurance during change.

Align Organizational Values

Where is the connect (or disconnect) between your employees' values and your organization's values—and why should it matter? Recent research found one in three workers report their employer's core values are not consistent with their own. "Management often seems to expect employees to ignore their personal values in favor of the ones posted on the wall. When employee values clash with the organization's operating values, the outcome is 'work avoidance'—passive, unproductive behaviors and a silent sabotage of projects and ideas."[48]

And on the positive side—when the values match? Jim Kouzes and Barry Posner explain the importance of shared values in the fourth edition of *The Leadership Challenge.*

> *Recognition of shared values provides people with a common language. Tremendous energy is generated when individual, group and organization values are in sync. Commitment, enthusiasm and drive are intensified. People have reasons for caring about their work.[49]*

Speaking of the values posted on the wall: have you noticed there is sometimes a difference between espoused values and practiced values?

The company values list hangs in the boardroom, the conference room and lunchroom. It's a great list, but I began to distrust it. The first sentence said, "We value employees more than anything else." I loved reading that when I first joined the company. I guess I loved finding a company where loyalty and commitment were a two-way street and highly valued. Now I don't believe in the list on the wall. We have regular lay-offs, mostly to deliver to shareholders. To be honest, the list should read, "We value shareholders more than anything else."

—Disenchanted (disengaged) employee

GO TO

Link
page 107

Talk with your employees about any values disconnects they feel. And help them identify where their values *do* align with the organization's. Corporate philanthropy or social responsibility programs can help create alignment. Link people to existing company projects, or support their finding or starting one themselves. If your talented people are proud of what their organization does in the community, their engagement levels can soar.

Values, You, and Your Team

We have looked at hundreds of transcripts from exit interviews. We were amazed at how many talented employees left because their values conflicted with those of their immediate supervisor or manager.

Tom's top value was clear to everyone—to his boss, his peers and his team. He valued bottom-line results and delivering on promises—at any cost, including frequent sacrifices in his personal life. He managed a group of Gen Ys who expected both a great job and a great life. After discussing the values gap in a staff meeting, Tom and his team realized they needed to get creative and to somehow reconcile the values gap between them. Here are the steps Tom took:

1. *Met with every team member to get clear about what mattered most to them.*

2. *Asked each of them to bring suggestions for closing the values gap to the next meeting.*

3. *Crafted tangible work agreements with each team member.*

4. *Agreed to discuss progress and revise agreements over the coming weeks and months.*

5. *Committed to keep working on it until the values gap was closed.*

One agreement entailed flexing the work schedule so an employee could attend his son's rugby matches. In another case, Tom clarified the performance objectives, gained agreement with the employee—then let go, allowing her to manage her own workload in her own way. One by one, Tom and his talented employees tested the new agreements, modified where necessary, and in time, closed the values gaps. It wasn't as difficult as Tom thought it would be—and it was worth the effort. His team is happier and more productive than ever before.

GO TO

Space
page 183

Are you aware of the values conflicts you may have with those on your team?

Sometimes as managers we tend to project our values onto our employees. But diversity of values will build strength in your team. Those who value creativity will be your innovators. Those who value independence will work productively for long stretches without prodding from you. Those who value order and routine will be your dependable, solid citizens. Don't try to make the solid citizen into a creative innovator. Recognize what each person values, and mine those values for the sake of the whole team. (Those who value perfection can be our copy editor.)

To Do

Consider talking about values with your team. Here is a set of questions that might get the conversation rolling, in any part of the globe:

★ What are the values we have individually? How are we similar? How are we different?

★ How might our differences get in the way?

★ Under what circumstances or pressures do we find our values colliding? Complementing?

★ What can we learn from someone whose values are different from our own?

★ Do we have espoused or practiced team values? How do they show up? Help us? Hinder us?

★ Should we spend a little time every meeting talking about where we're "on" or "off" our values? If not, why not?

Bottom Line

The match between your employees' values and the organization's or team's values is a powerful factor in keeping good people. How satisfied are your talented people with their everyday tasks? Do you know enough about your employees' values to answer that question? Values may be difficult to uncover, but they are worth the effort. They are powerful forces in an employee's decision to stay or leave. Imagine your employees as your customers. Now, what do they value most? How can you help them attain it?

TWENTY-THREE

Wellness

SUSTAIN IT

Ponder this: Are they sick or tired?

Does your organization insist on yearly physicals? Does it invest in gymnasiums, volleyball courts, or stress management workshops? If you're laughing, keep reading. Companies that take wellness seriously find that the payoff is great, not only in retention, but also in energy for the job and in productivity. But this chapter is not about what the corporation can do. We are interested in how you, the manager, can enhance your team's wellness.

One manager in Dublin suggested *walking desks*[50] as a way for his employees to get and stay fit. Some thought it was a joke—but he was serious! Another manager in Spain transformed a closet into the perfect space for a much-needed *power nap*. She was happy to report that in Spain the siesta is still alive and well and so are her employees! Daily naps have been shown

to correlate with lower coronary mortality and greater long-term health.[51] Makes you want to take a nap, doesn't it?

What are *you* doing to encourage the wellness of your talented people?

Wellness and Survival of the Fit

Today's workplace is typically high-energy and highly productive. To play successfully within it, you and your employees must be *well and fit*, mentally, emotionally, and physically. In this competitive environment, wellness is a "must have" rather than a "nice to have." Without it, you simply will not win. By focusing on your employees' wellness, you can increase the odds that they will stay and play effectively on your team.

What Is Wellness?

To one person, wellness means that he can enter the Dead Sea Marathon and finish in four hours. To another, it may mean finally being free of migraine headaches. To another, it may mean slimming down or reducing stress and high blood pressure before the next physical exam.

GO TO
_____
Understand
page 206

We define wellness as a *state of physical, mental, and emotional fitness*. Some might call it *well-being*. To capture a clear picture of it, you might need to think back to a recent vacation when you felt incredibly relaxed, physically healthy and energetic, mentally sharp (maybe even creative), and emotionally satisfied. It may seem unreasonable to expect that you or your employees will feel at work like you feel on vacation, but it is useful to have the "perfect world" scenario in mind as you strive to increase your employees' fitness and wellness levels.

Show interest in your employees' well-being. Here's what we are talking about.

Alas (almost)

Tanya had recently missed several days of work and seemed uncharacteristically quiet and distant at her job. She was typically vivacious and fun-loving, and she often cheered up other team members with sagging spirits. Tanya was still getting her work done, so her manager resisted saying anything to her about her absences or the shifts in her mood. Besides, he was concerned that to question her might somehow be crossing a line from the work world to the private world, and that seemed risky to him. So he said nothing.

Three months later Tanya tearfully handed her manager her resignation. He was shocked and told her that he did not want her to go, that he and the entire team valued her highly. She seemed surprised by his response and said so. "I thought you didn't care about me at all, since you never asked why I was missing work or why I seemed so sad when I did show up. I assumed that the team would be better off without me."

Tanya's boss finally did what she had wanted him to do weeks earlier. He did not pry but just offered to help. Tanya began to cry (this time with gratitude) and explained that she was having health problems and that her responsibilities as a mother and a member of his team were just more than she could handle. She said that it was the stress of balancing everything that was getting her down, not the illness itself.

Within minutes, a talented employee's resignation turned into a plan for how Tanya would manage her work and family responsibilities while she regained her health. The plan included working from home two days a week, as well as beginning work earlier in the morning and going home early in the afternoon. Tanya's loyalty and commitment to her boss and her team skyrocketed, her productivity remained high, and within a few months she was back on her original schedule and feeling great.

Tanya's boss did the right thing just in time for Tanya, the team, and himself. He asked what he could do and then brainstormed solutions with his valuable employee. You can bet that Tanya will not be easily enticed away to a new team or opportunity. The only thing he could have done better would have been to talk to her earlier.

Whether your employee faces a physical problem, stress, or an emotional challenge, your response as a manager can be consistent: ask how you can help and then collaborate on a plan.

To Do

★ Notice if something is wrong or if your employees' work habits change dramatically. Do not wait. Ask if there is anything you can do to help. How simple it seems and how few managers do this.

One of my most talented engineers was having major temper flare-ups and causing a lot of turmoil on the team. My boss suggested I fire him. I decided that this employee was important enough to invest in. We talked, and I referred him to the Employee Assistance Program, where he got the help he needed. He has dealt with whatever was bothering him and is a joy to work with again. My supporting him through this proved to be an important statement to him and also to the team. We are stronger and more productive than ever.

—Engineering manager

★ When an employee does tell you what is wrong, partner with that person to create a plan to remedy the situation.

The "B" Word (Balance)

Most of us need a job, and all of us want a life. We should be able to have both.

A senior executive lamented, "I haven't called my mother in a month, and I'm six months overdue for a mammogram. Both issues weigh on my mind and increase my stress." Workers want a break, and they want a life outside work. They want time to call Mom and get a checkup.

Balance between work and personal life contributes to wellness and constantly challenges the wellness-minded manager. One team we know has spent so much time in recent years dealing with the issue of balance that they now call it the "B" word. It is almost off-limits as a discussion topic because it seems there are few solutions, and they have become "sick of talking about it."

We believe, though, that you *need to talk about it*—and think about it—and even do something about it! What does balance (some call it work/life integration) mean to you and to your employees? (It is different for everyone.)

One plant manager we heard about gives each of the 90 members of his team a small amount of money each year to do something (anything!) to bring balance into their lives. His only request: "Tell me how you've used the money." The ways in which employees spend the money underscore how individual our balance needs are. Employees report spending their money on ballroom dance lessons, a drum set, gardening tools, and instruction in tai chi and kickboxing. The manager doesn't spend a lot of money, and the message he sends is crystal-clear. Do you have a discretionary budget that you might spend this way?

We are not suggesting that your employees' balance issues are your concern alone or that you must provide the answers. We are suggesting, however, that you can take actions to encourage balance and thus wellness.

> *Imagine life as a game in which you are juggling five balls in the air. You name them—work, family, health, friends, and spirit—you're keeping all of these in the air. You will soon understand that work is a rubber ball. If you drop it, it will bounce back. But the other four balls—family, health, friends, and spirit—are made of glass. If you drop one of these, it will be irrevocably scuffed, marked, nicked, damaged, or even shattered. It will never be the same. You must understand that.*
>
> —Brian Dyson, former CEO of Coca-Cola

Overwhelm Is an Understatement

The pressures to do more with less. Move faster than the competition. Be more creative, more innovative, more distinct. Do it with fewer dollars. Be available at all times. These pressures push many to say that work just asks too much.

In the United States and many other parts of the world (e.g., Thailand, Korea, Pakistan), the work week keeps getting longer, usually in the hopes of creating a competitive advantage. That's in spite of decades of research that confirm that "the *sweet spot* is 40 hours a week—and that while adding another 20 hours provides a minor increase in productivity, that increase only lasts for three to four weeks, and then turns negative." The good news is that in 6 of the top 10 most competitive countries in the world (Sweden, Finland, Germany, the Netherlands, Denmark, and the UK), it's *illegal* to demand more than a 48-hour workweek.[52]

Alas

Kumar has noticed that he has been snapping at his employees, having trouble sleeping, and feeling generally sluggish. When a friend asked him how he was spending his time away from work, he answered, "What time away from work?" He used to spend evenings at home and had enjoyed movies, friends, books, and music to relax. He worked out at the gym four nights a week. All of that seems a distant memory now. His new boss has set the tone: those who are even remotely ambitious or committed to the organization work late every night. So much for balance and wellness. Kumar's employees are fed up with his grumpiness (two have recently quit). Kumar's productivity has dropped, he has constant headaches, and he feels increasing resentment toward his boss and the organization. Recently Kumar has begun to check out Internet job postings, thinking that there must be a saner place to work! He'll be gone soon, having found a workplace where balance is at least a topic of discussion and where his boss expects that people have a life outside work.

So what about you? What example do you set as a manager, and what do you expect from your people? Ask yourself these questions:

- Do I promote workaholism? Am I a workaholic?

- Do I expect my employees to travel or work on weekends? How often?

- Do I hold numerous early morning or early evening meetings?

- Do I compliment employees for their long hours or, instead, for the quality work they complete?

How did you do? Often managers discourage balance by the examples they set or by what they expect and reward.

To Do

★ *Set the example you want them to follow.* If you want them to have more balance in their lives, you have to model it. Share what you do to achieve balance in your life. Your employees may think that you have none. (We hope they're wrong.)

★ *Hold a balance discussion* at your next staff meeting (or in one-on-one meetings). Dedicate the whole meeting to the topic.

★ *Ask people what they juggle* in their lives and what matters most to them. (Be ready to hear that work is *not the number one priority* for many of them.)

★ *Support your employees in achieving balance.* Encourage the activities that they love; ask about their golf lessons or their children's school plays.

Stretched and Stressed

I used up all my sick days so I called in dead.

—*Anonymous*

Hans Selye, the founder of the field of stress management, said, "To be free of stress is to be dead." We agree that just *living* is often stressful. But Selye and others have found that, although optimum levels of stress produce peak performance, overdoses can definitely lead to poor performance and even to illness.

In organizations, we seldom see too little stress. We sometimes see the optimum stress level and high performance results. Most often, however, we see stress overload and negative results on health and on productivity. There seems to be a high correlation between lack of balance and stress. Where balance is missing, the workload typically appears to be very high and stressful. When people have balanced lives, they seem to have less work stress, or they just manage it better.

For 40 years, we focused, as a medical profession, on the deleterious effects of stress. We now know that with people who are stressed, there is a direct correlation with addictive behavior, cardiovascular disease, infections and some types of cancer. But we hadn't looked at the opposite. If stress could make you sick, could happiness make you better? And the evidence shows it can.[53]

—*Dr. Deepak Chopra*

Both Switzerland and France have labor laws that protect employees' health and wellness. Swiss law prescribes the "duty of care," where companies are not allowed to accept or create a work environment that is hostile to employees' health. Meanwhile, French employers must ensure the physical and mental health of employees. This includes taking measures against any psychological suffering and stress. Employers must therefore remove unrealistic deadlines and heavy workloads. In turn, they must ensure that employees have control over their own workloads and schedules.

Perhaps you manage in a country that has no such laws. There are still many ways that you, as an individual manager, can promote a healthy work environment. Here are a few:

To Do

★ Watch for signs of excess stress. When you think you see it in your employees, ask them how they are doing (or feeling). They will appreciate your asking and may confide in you.

★ Once you know what's going on, brainstorm possible solutions with your employees. Be open and willing to think creatively as you search for ways to relieve stress and increase well-being.

★ Support your employees as they practice stress management. For example, if Mike decides he needs to take two 15-minute brisk walks during the day to relieve stress, be sure that you reward his actually doing it. Your support will pay off.

★ Take a good look at the role you play. Stop calling your employees in the evening—give them a break.

When we create a desirable workplace and find good ways to have work-life balance, we'll attract and we'll retain the best people—and that's our competitive advantage.

—*Lewis Platt, former CEO, Hewlett-Packard*

Small Steps to Big Change

Try some of these stress busters. You go first—then pass on the ideas to your talented people:

- Shift some of the work to others if possible. Think about who could help and how to ask for the help.

- Take more breaks. Get up; move around; go for a quick walk.

- Take a break from "electronic leashes"—declare a smart-phone-free Wednesday morning (unless that increases their stress!).

- Learn relaxation, visualization, or breathing techniques. Take a stress management or mindfulness class.

- Exercise as a way to relieve stress. Join a gym or take up power walking, yoga or jogging.

- Implement "no meetings on Fridays." Think of the work you could get done!

- Seek professional help or counseling.

- Sleep and eat. How long has it been since you took a lunch break—away from your desk?

Take a vacation—a real one. One manager we know tells his people not to check voice mail or e-mail! (Yes, that means you'd need to have backup support.)

Bottom Line

Savvy managers view work/life balance and stress reduction initiatives as strategic business tools, not as employee perks. If your employees are well and feel a balance between work and life outside work, you are far more likely to have a well-functioning organization. Your best employees will work hard, produce for you, *and stick around* in an environment that promotes their emotional, mental, and physical health and fitness.

TWENTY-FOUR

X-ers and others

HANDLE WITH CARE

Ponder this: How are they different?

WARNING!

This chapter contains generalizations that reflect research into the attitudes and behaviors of the age groups now in the workforce. We recommend that you manage each of your employees according to their individual characteristics, while taking these generalizations into account. We want to give you potentially useful information about patterns that fall within generational lines. Our intent is not to label people but to offer guidelines for your thinking so you can keep your best people.

Does your organization invest in researching your customers' demographics? Consumer research specialists and marketing experts use that knowledge to better serve or sell their product or service. Wouldn't it make sense to use that same kind of proactive approach for understanding your own people?

The primary value of generational analysis is to make the actions of others a little more understandable. By understanding other generations' perspectives, we are better able to position our ideas and request in ways that are likely to have positive results and avoid at least some of the frustrations of today's workplace.

Perhaps my most important suggestion is simply to remember that the way something looks to you is probably not the way it looks to others. Looking at the situation through others' lenses will give you a clue about why they do what they do. As you work with people from other generations and other backgrounds, think about their formative years for clues about why they may see things differently than you do.[54]

—*Tamara Erickson, author of* What's Next, Gen X?

Here's an example of using generational knowledge to deliver what your employees want:

Assumption: Your talented workers, of any age, want flexibility. Here's how the generations might think about and define *flexibility* differently from one another. Notice the nuances, based on stage of life, values, and expectations.

GO TO

Space
page 183

Flexibility

- *Matures*—I've *earned* it. I want time to spend with grandchildren (or great-grandchildren), take more vacations, learn something new, or have time off to test this thing called retirement.

- *Boomers*—I *want* it. I want more balance in my life (finally) and flextime to spend with kids, aging parents, and grandkids. I want to take a trip to Europe, and I want to give back to my community in a meaningful way.

- *X-ers*—I *deserve* it. I want flexibility to do the work my way. I want to be able to choose between taking that management class or spending the time with friends, family, or hobbies.

- **Ys**—I *expect* it. I want a sabbatical to live in Japan for a year. I want the freedom to go to lunch with colleagues and come back when we want to.

They all want flexibility, but their definitions of flexibility differ strikingly.

What's a Generation, and Who Are They?

Note: If you work outside of the United States, you might have different generational birth years and names from those you see in this chapter. What we all have in common, though, is generational differences in the workplace. As you read this chapter, think about how the characteristics of different age groups impact how work gets done in your organization.

A *generation* is a group of people who share birth years and therefore share life stages. Generations are defined by spikes and declines in birthrates. The people in those groups are influenced by the cultural events, changes, and challenges that they experience, especially during their formative years. As a result, they bring their own set of attitudes, perceptions, and values to the workplace.

> *To be part of a generation is much more than the simple matter of your birthday. It's to be a part of an era. It's to have fallen in love with a rock band and not a big band. Or to have played ball with an aluminum bat instead of a wooden one. It's to have done things as no other generation would.*
>
> *—Unknown*

Today's workplace contains four distinct generations, each bringing its unique perspective and expectations. No wonder we have plenty of opportunities for generation gaps! The birth dates and population of each group varies slightly, depending on whose research you are using. We used *American Generations: Who They Are, How They Live, What They Think* by Susan Mitchell.[55]

We suggest you worry less about the generational labels or dates and, instead, ask yourself, "How are they different—or similar? And how can that knowledge help me keep them?"

To Do

As you read this chapter, ponder these questions. Then discuss them with your team or business unit. Be sure to include representatives from each generation, if possible. Thanks to The Learning Café for letting us use them![56]

★ How is each generation in our work unit unique? What special capabilities does each generation have to contribute?

★ What captures each generation's attention about our work environment?

★ What generations are represented among our current and future customers?

★ What generations are represented among our current and future employees?

★ To be "generation-friendly," what should we stop doing? Start doing? Continue doing?

★ What can we do to bridge generational communication issues in our workplace?

★ What policies, practices, and initiatives should we be looking at through generational "lenses"?

Generations at Work

	Matures	Boomers	Gen X	Gen Y
Born	1933-1945	1946-1964	1965-1976	1977-1998
1930				2000
	34 Million	76 Million	41 Million	75 Million

Millennials/Generation Y (1977–1998)

Gen Ys are also known as the Nexters and the Echo Boomers. In the United States, there are approximately 75 million people in this group, and they promise to have as great an impact on the workplace as the similarly sized Boomer generation.

Globally, it is the largest generation yet, although its relative size varies wide-ly. In many parts of Asia, Ys are significantly greater in number than members of older generations, while in Europe, due to slowing birth rates, they are fewer in number than the generations that preceded them. Coupled with the generation's sheer overall size, Ys' often surprisingly different approaches to work make them well worth watching. This is a generation we can all learn from if we suspend our own views about the way things should be done.

Tamara Erickson, author of What's Next, Gen X?

They're the summer interns, recent college grads, and new MBAs. Many are on their second job. In fact, since they tend to "job hop," they *could* already be on their third or fourth job! They could be your assistant or your boss. The first of this group have now been in the workplace long enough for us to get a feel for who they are and what they want.

They're ambitious, they're demanding, and they question everything, so if there isn't a good reason for that long commute or late night, don't expect them to do it. When it comes to loyalty, the companies they work for are last on their list—behind their families, their friends, their communities, their coworkers, and, of course, themselves.

What They Bring and What They Want

Gen Ys are digital natives. They've grown up with cell phones, laptops, broadband, and their own digital social networks. They not only have "tricked-out" PCs; they have servers—to run a second business, if desired. They are great multitaskers. Just watch them do homework while they chat on their cell phones, answer e-mail, stream online TV shows, and message their MySpace.com or Facebook.com buddies. They're hard workers and used to meeting high expectations. They appreciate structure, process, and feedback.

Simply waving money in the faces of Gen Y as a hiring tool is often a futile effort. What makes a job truly hot is more about flexibility, freedom, and development than just cold cash. They want the money, but on their own terms: good hours, a good work climate, and a job that offers opportunities to learn, grow, and have real responsibilities.

Bottom line: they want *cool,* leading-edge careers that make a difference in the world.

Many prefer group activities to individual pursuits. They're great team players. They are tolerant of authority, welcome diversity, and are the best-educated generation in U.S. history. This group is also the best prepared for globalization. They've always had access to world news (CNN was born about the same time they were), they've loved Pokémon cards along with kids from Japan, they've found a McDonald's restaurant in every country they've visited, and they have surely communicated with people from other countries on the Net, one way or another.

Gen Ys are civic minded, intellectually curious, and polite. They are drawn to the Matures, who can offer great mentor/reverse-mentor relationships. A Chinese colleague said that younger workers there greatly respect the older generation. There is a saying, "家有一老，如有一宝," which means "Having an elderly person at home is like having a treasure." Having that treasure at work is a gift!

Hints for Hanging On

Remember to ask each Gen Y what will keep him or her. Take A through Z into account, but be sure to include these strategies:

- *Opportunities*—Find ways for them to exercise their intellectual curiosity and work in teams. They're used to being challenged and structured, so invite them to dive in and co-create their next assignment or promotional opportunity. Be sure to give them the technology they are used to. They're already dependent on it. They also respond to additional (paid) time off.

- *Truth*—Give them regular, honest feedback. They've been raised on schedules, tests, and constant input from tutors, teachers, parents, and coaches, all working to build excellence. They want more than the annual performance appraisal.

- **Goals**—Help them create stretch goals, multiple career options, and a sense of job security. And remember to reward them when they achieve the goals, in ways that matter most to them (recognition, day off, bonus, latest technology).

Generation X (1965–1976)

Since the first edition of *Love 'Em or Lose 'Em,* this group has grown up. They were the new kids on the block then, and now they're becoming pretty entrenched in middle management. We've had a chance to work with them, manage them, and report to them. They're not a mystery anymore.

There are 41 million of them in the United States, and they are the wellspring of management talent that is expected to take over as the Boomers exit the workplace. There aren't enough of them to do that job. X-ers will be stretched thin (yes, even thinner than today), and they'll have multiple options as organizations compete for their talent.

What They Bring and What They Want

When older workers look at an X-er's résumé, they often conclude "a job hopper." The work history may look fragmented to an older hiring manager but makes perfect sense to the X-er. For X-ers, an organization is a place to learn new skills and build experience, a springboard to a new opportunity there or elsewhere. Many X-ers' résumés reflect this perspective, showing five or six jobs within as many years. When they join you, many of them bring a breadth of experience that will strengthen your team.

Gen-X-ers bring an independent approach to their work. They want to clearly understand what's expected; but once expectations are established and deliverables are defined, they need to have space, resources, and the freedom to produce the desired results, in their own way and in their own time.

The pay was good. The location was great. But I knew I could do much more. They wanted me to keep doing what I was doing. So I left.

—X-er in a high-tech company

While the X-ers do not offer "blind" loyalty to a company, they can be fiercely loyal to a project, a team, a boss they like, the mission of the organization, and, yes, even the organization itself. But that loyalty is based on mutuality. As long as they are challenged, growing, enjoying the work, and getting recognized for their contributions—and as long as you are getting what you want and need from them—they'll stay. When that partnership weakens or the scales tip to one side, they'll be outta there!

They also want balance between work and their personal lives. They have boundaries, and they use those boundaries effectively. That doesn't mean they won't put in the occasional all-nighter when it's needed. But don't expect they'll do that for the next 20 years. Many feel that one of the greatest gifts of this generation to the rest of us is introducing the expectation of work/life balance. They don't live to work. They work to live.

Hints for Hanging On

Just as each generation has unique characteristics, so, too, does every member of that generation. Remember to ask all your talented people what will keep them. Then keep these strategies in mind:

- **Careers**—Keep them challenged, learning, and progressing. They see your workplace as a stop along the way and a place to build their portfolio of skills and a strong résumé. Help them develop new skills and identify career options in your organization.

- **Information**—Keep them in the loop. Communicate early, honestly, and often, in ways that work for them. E-mail is a favorite for this generation, but face-to-face will build the relationship and increase the odds of keeping them.

- **Space**—Provide flexibility, freedom, and work/life balance. Do not micromanage these people. Find out what kind of freedom they value most and how they can increase balance in their lives. (If you're from an older generation, take a lesson from them on this one!)

Some readers have said to us, "Wait—I'm a Boomer and I want the same things X-ers want." This is probably true. Here's the difference: If Boomers don't get these things, they'll whine around the water cooler. If X-ers don't get them, they'll walk! While their wants may not differ greatly from those of other employees, X-ers are more willing to say what they want and to leave if you don't deliver.

Baby Boomers (1946–1964)

There are 76 million people in this generation, sometimes divided into two groups: the early Boomers and the late Boomers. "King and queen of the corporate hill," Boomers are competitive and hardworking. Their focus on personal goals and achievement has been the hallmark of their generation. And now, as they approach the traditional retirement age, Boomers are beginning to question the meaning and purpose of their lives—again. Some are part of the "sandwich generation," raising kids and caring for aging parents at the same time. Others, whose children are grown and gone, have more time on their hands and plenty of disposable income. They're wondering how and when they'll find the time to enjoy it!

What They Bring and What They Want

Boomers have a driven, "get it done at all costs" attitude that has made them phenomenally successful. At the same time, that attitude often conflicts with the two younger generations, who see Boomers as having sacrificed everything, including family life, for their own achievement and self-fulfillment.

Boomers have been called the "me" generation and accused of being self-absorbed. On the other hand, they see the attitudes of the two younger generations as an unwillingness to "pay their dues" and "earn their stripes."

Now, they're looking for balance and a way out. They're pondering early retirement, but they don't necessarily intend to stop working. The question is, what kind of work will they be doing, and can they do that work for you?

Hints for Hanging On

Try these strategies to increase the odds of engaging and retaining your Boomers. Don't forget to ask what they want next.

- **Passion**—Help them find meaningful work. They've been looking for meaning in their work and lives since they were ten. Ask what they're passionate about, what some of their current interests are, and how they might blend those passions with their work. Ask, too, what new role they might like to play. They still have plenty of energy and time left to contribute to your team.

- **Enrich**—Keep them on their cutting edge. Teach them. They still want to learn, even the oldest of them. Visit a junior college and notice the silver hair in the world history, pottery, and political science classes. Ask what new thing they'd like to learn this coming year.

- **Reward**—Notice and thank them for their dedication and commitment. They're annoyed with the Gen Xs' and Gen Ys' apparent disinterest in loyalty, commitment, and a work-'til-you-drop mentality. They want you to acknowledge those values and characteristics, and if you do, they'll continue to give you their all.

Matures/Silent Generation (1933–1945)

Wait—aren't they gone already? Maybe from your organization. But many people of this generation and older are still working—in large and small companies, in entrepreneurial ventures, and even in brand-new ways.

A 93-year-old employee at Vita Needle said, "Age discrimination abounds here—the older the better." With an average employee age of 74, this organization has mastered the art of hiring, engaging, and retaining a phenomenal workforce. When asked why they hired such mature people, one manager said, "They bring attention to detail, eagerness to learn, commitment to quality, and loyalty. Who wouldn't want that?"

Vita Needle might be unique—but they might also be a trendsetter!

Matures are also known as Veterans, the Swing Generation, the Silents, and Pre-Boomers. The United States has 34 million people in this generation. Rich with work experience, they built many traditional corporations through their hard work and loyalty. They appreciate and understand the importance of achieving common goals and offer a lasting knowledge legacy. For many reasons, you may want them to stay a little while longer, even in a part-time or advisory capacity.

What They Bring and What They Want

Matures lead your company, retain your customers, and carry your institutional memories. They are civic minded and helping oriented. And they have a significant knowledge legacy, if only someone will remember to tap into it.

In the movie About Schmidt, *Jack Nicholson sits at his desk, watching the clock tick toward 5 p.m. on his last day of work. He's retiring. His life's work at this company now seems to reside in a pile of boxes in his cleaned-out office. He keeps asking people, "When are they coming for the boxes?" Five o'clock comes. It's time for Schmidt to leave his office for the final time. And the boxes sit there. No one came to get them.*

Schmidt knew they could benefit by his experience, if only they took the time to listen—to learn from him.

Hints for Hanging On

Remember to ask each Mature what will keep him or her. Consider using some of these strategies:

- *Dignity*—Respect and mine their knowledge. Tell them how much you value what they bring to you, the team, and the organization. Then, really *use* what they bring!

- *Mentor*—Let them mentor younger workers and pass on their wisdom and knowledge. With more similarities than any other two generations, the combination of a Mature and a Gen Y makes for a great mentoring (and reverse-mentoring) relationship.

  The company will be in for a real eye-opening as the older workforce is released. No one is teaching the intangibles of the job. You can teach an employee what a pump is and how it works—but not what it sounds like when it's going bad.

  —Oil company employee

- *Link*—Connect them to the community as a way of leveraging their expertise. Ask if they'd like to serve on your organization's community service committee or head up the next charity drive.

And, here's one more:

- *Hire*—When you start running short on talent, or you want someone smart, loyal, hardworking, and connected to your customers, consider hiring a Mature, even if only in a part-time position. Many organizations are now partnering with AARP to match job-seeking senior workers with the right employers. It's a win-win.

Now you have enough theory. Let's try applications.

Clash Avoidance

I hired a young, talented woman with a master's degree in communications. After working for us for just a year, she asked for time off—and not just for a vacation. She asked for a one-year break to take a job as Cinderella in Disneyland, Japan. I talked it over with my boss, and we decided to give her an unpaid sabbatical. She is so talented, and we want her back. I feel confident she'll come back and hope she will spend many years working with us.

—Manager, public relations firm

This manager could have considered her request absurd, based on the fact that he (a Boomer) *never* would have asked for a year-long sabbatical after one year with a company. Instead, he took generational differences into account and then valued this employee enough to explore the possibilities with her. Can you do that?

Here are a few other culture clashes we've heard about:

- The hiring manager (a Boomer) is interviewing a Gen Y (age 28). When he asks the candidate what questions she might have, she answers, "How much vacation will I get, and when can I take the first one?"

- A Gen X-er says no thanks to a "mandatory" training class. He tells his Boomer boss that he plans to use a mentor and read a book on the topic instead.

- A Gen Y reports to a Gen X who is an "absentee manager."

- An X-er tells his Mature boss that he has to leave to attend his son's soccer match, even though the project isn't done.

- A Boomer wants to "brief" a Gen Y before she goes to meet a longtime customer. She says, "No, thanks, we'll do fine."

Do these ring a bell for you? How would you stop, think, and avoid a clash, knowing what you now know?

I do not like this person. I must get to know him better.

—*Abraham Lincoln*

Here's a cheat sheet that might help you remember some of the generational differences. (Thanks again, Learning Café.) Use it to better engage all members of your workforce![57]

	Millennials/ Gen Y	Gen X	Boomers	Matures/ Silent
Climate Here's how work fits into our lives	Lifestyle, work style	Work to live	Live to work	Work first, then play
Create work climate by being a boss who is . . .	Coach, mentor and friend	Hands-off	Collaborative	Respectful and in charge
Communication Tune in to communication methods	Text me	Send an e-mail	Have a meeting	Put it in writing
Pay attention to feedback preferences	Tell me nice and tell me now	How am I doing?	Show me the money	No news is good news
Career Our generation's career motto is . . .	"I want it all now!"	"What can the organization do for me?"	"Pay your dues."	"Just do the work."
Build your career success by . . .	Moving on to the next thing quickly	Developing a portable skill portfolio	Climbing the ladder	Earning a fair day's pay for fair day's work

Talent-focused managers will be aware of all these differences and use them appropriately to develop, engage, and retain their talent.

Gen Z (1999–present)

Just when you thought you were done, there's a new generation on the way (as there always is) and, unless you're ready to retire, you'll be working with them. They're also called the "I" generation or the Net generation.

In some European countries, there is talk about this group being the "lost generation." At the writing of this book, the unemployment rate for employees under 25 is tremendously high in Greece, Spain, Italy, Portugal, and Ireland. These young adults might be well trained and educated but have slim chances of finding jobs in their own countries. If the trend continues, we'll see a Gen Z migration within Europe, mostly from South to North, over the coming years.

The experts are placing their bets on what this group will be like in the workforce. Here's a sneak peak at a few of the characteristics Gen Z-ers are expected to bring to work. They will

- be bright—supposedly the smartest generation to date.

- be the "real" digital natives and the most wired generation ever.

- communicate quickly—forget email!

- be open to new ideas.

- enjoy social circles that include people from different ethnic groups, races and religions.

- bring back individualism, preferring not to do everything with a team.

- be self-directed and focused on their own goals.

- process information at lightning speed, act and produce quickly.

- respond best to a manager who is flexible and goal oriented and who gives frequent but short-term milestones. (Got that?)

Sounds good? Now we'll wait and see.

Bottom Line

The challenge of motivating and retaining our multigenerational workforce will continue. Learn about their differences, not to separate them but to understand them better and work with them more effectively. Use A to Z strategies with all, but keep in mind those that appear to matter most to each generation. And remember that retention is essentially an individual activity. Find out what each of your talented employees wants, regardless of his or her generation.

TWENTY-FIVE

POWER DOWN

Ponder this: Do you believe your way is the only way?

Think about being on a highway on-ramp in a busy city, at an intersection with no stop signs, or in a line forming at the movies. When someone says, "No, *you* go first," with a smile and gesture, you may think how remarkable and rare that action is.

Similarly, in many workplaces, yielding is all too rare. It could be because managers want to hang on to their power and prestige once they finally have it. Or perhaps they've never had a manager who empowered them, so they're not sure how it works. They may have learned to micromanage from the boss who never seemed to trust them, looked over their shoulders and closely inspected every aspect of the work—as they did it.

Our study of exit interviews (why people leave) reveals that micromanagement does not work for most talented employees. Yielding does work. When you yield occasionally to your employees, you empower them to think for themselves, to be more creative, more enthusiastic, and probably more productive. Your employees' enthusiasm and sense of value as team members will increase the odds that they will stay engaged and stick around.

"Power Down? I Just Got Powered Up!"

A sense of newly found power is one of the joys of being promoted into a leadership role. Even if you were never consciously looking to be more powerful, it may be ego gratifying to be anointed as skilled enough to make bigger decisions, direct others' activities, and even take the spotlight bows for team successes.

Once you receive that kind of power, it might be difficult to give some away. Many of our role models taught us to hang on to that power—to wield it fairly (the benevolent dictator type)—but never to give it away. Then management books in the 1980s proclaimed empowerment, and with it came confusion for many managers, who asked, "Why should I let my employees make more decisions, take more credit, be in charge? And once you tell me why, tell me *how* to empower my people."

> *Ignore me as needed to get your job done.*
> —*Sign on VP's door, courtesy of Liz Wiseman, author of* Multipliers

So let's take a look at these two critical questions: why yield and how can you yield?

Why Yield? What's in It for You?

This case study highlights several benefits of yielding.

Alas *Veronika, a manager in a global drug research and development company, woke up one morning and recognized that 20 percent of her employees were doing 80 percent of the thinking. She was concerned for a number of reasons:*

- *The 80 percent of her employees who weren't really using their creative and intellectual abilities also seemed to be disengaged or just going through the motions at work. Their job satisfaction level seemed low, and in many cases she knew they could be more productive if they were more involved somehow in the work.*

- *The competition would gain an edge if her company didn't use talent better, get more creative, and stay on the cutting edge.*

- *She and a handful of thinking employees were overstretched and spent much of their time answering questions and meeting with others to solve their problems.*

- *She had lost some talented employees and learned in the exit interviews that they were not being challenged enough and had grown bored.*

What is wrong with this picture?

Veronika knew she needed to

- leverage the brilliance and creativity in her group;

- get people more engaged in their work;

- increase job satisfaction and all the benefits connected to it (like productivity);

- free up her time—and that of some of her other *thinking* employees—spent answering questions and making decisions for others; and

- retain her talent!

Veronika knew she had to do something to meet these goals. It took her a while to realize that her solution was right in front of her all the time. We'll look at what Veronika did to solve her problem in a minute. For now, look at your situation.

To Do

Check out this list:

★ Is your organization lean and mean, like so many others after years of downsizing?

★ Is your span of control larger than ever and are the expectations from above constantly increasing your workload and pressure?

★ Do some of your employees seem apathetic or less than eager to show up on Monday mornings?

★ Are many of your employees still waiting to be told what to do every step of the way?

★ Is the competition nipping at your heels?

★ Have you lost any of your talented team members because they were bored or needed a new challenge?

GO TO

Opportunities
page 138

If your answers are no, then either you are already yielding power to your employees, or you aren't yet feeling the pressure to do so. If either of these is true, move on to another chapter to focus on something that matters more right now or that you may not already be doing quite as well.

If you answered yes to four or more on the checklist, then read on. You have just identified the reasons to power down. You must yield to your people to compete successfully. And you must yield in order to keep your talented employees on your team.

The higher up you go in an organization, the more you need to let other people be the winners and not make it all about winning yourself. For bosses, that means being careful about how you hand out encouragement. If you find yourself saying, "Great ideas, but…," try cutting your response off at "ideas."

—Marshall Goldsmith, executive coach

Who's Got the Right of Way?

You may be convinced that you could benefit by giving more power to your employees, yet find it difficult to know where to start. The rules can be fuzzy or hard to remember, just like the road rules that guide merging into a roundabout or crossing an intersection that has no stop signs.

In the matter of powering down to your employees, the uncertainty is even greater because *there are no rules.* Your organization establishes cultural norms and role models, but as an individual manager you have tremendous leeway to give power.

Let's take another look at the case study to see how Veronika yielded.

Alas Revisited

Veronika realized that she needed to get at least 80 percent of her people doing the thinking, not 20 percent. She analyzed why they waited for direction, came to her for answers, and basically let their brains take extended breaks day after day. One conclusion was shocking: she was a big part of the problem.

Veronika had been promoted because she was bright and a good leader. It was incredibly gratifying to be given more people to manage, a large budget, and her own office. She encouraged her people to come to her anytime with their problems and questions. Veronika felt important and brilliant as she repeatedly solved day-to-day problems that her employees brought her. (Ever felt like that?) It dawned on her that she had been rewarding their "sleepy brain syndrome." Why should they think if she would do it for them?

So Veronika did just one thing to power down. She hung a sign on her door that looked like this:

ANSWERS

What? That's it? End of story? Well, yes, basically. Veronika explained to her employees that she had been underserving and undervaluing them by answering all of their questions and giving them step-by-step direction. She admitted to them that she had also robbed the organization of tremendous intellectual and creative capital by giving answers instead of asking questions. So when people came through her open door and asked their questions as they always had, she pointed to the sign and asked them powerful, thought-provoking questions like these:

- What do you think the problem is?

- Who do you think should be involved in solving this issue?

- What are the choices we have?

These questions empowered people to solve problems creatively, to lean on each other instead of on the boss, and to come up with multiple options. She gave encouragement and praise as people struggled to produce outstanding, creative solutions and new approaches. Her team's productivity and retention rates surpassed all others in the organization. Other managers came to her to find out what she was doing to magically inspire such phenomenal results.

Veronika chuckled as she related the secret of her success. "I had to set aside my ego. I could not be the all-knowing sage if I wanted my employees' brains to keep functioning. I truly had to yield to them, to accept them as brilliant, eager-to-succeed colleagues. I had to power down, give them some of my previously guarded power and importance. The result is that we all win. My job is easier and more gratifying and our results are the best ever. The best part is my most talented people are happier and more motivated than ever before and they plan to stick around as long as the fun continues."

There is more to Veronika's approach than meets the eye. The "No Answers" sign could be an annoyance if the follow-through did not include key elements:

- ***Trust your employees to come up with the answers.*** Even if you would have done it another way, consider the approaches they create and support them all the way.

   A manager at a food manufacturing plant yielded to his assembly-line workers. They developed a schedule and a new team system that boosted production, reduced overhead costs and downtime, and improved recruitment and retention.

- ***Manage your reactions when you yield and they crash!*** Powering down and yielding are sometimes risky, and failures will happen. Instead of punishing, collaborate with your empowered employees to learn from the mistake. Focus on what they could do differently next time around, rather than the rearview mirror approach of what they should have done.

   A senior manager made a mistake that cost his company $10 million. As he walked into his boss's office, he anticipated anger and most probably a firing. His boss asked him what he had learned from the mistake, and he quickly listed all the things he would do differently next time. Then he waited for the ax to fall. And he waited. Finally, he asked, "Aren't you going to fire me?" The boss answered, "Why would I fire you? I just invested $10 million in your learning."

- ***Serve your employees.*** Be a resource to them. Yielding doesn't mean you take the next exit. Empowerment spells disaster in too many cases where the manager tosses decisions and workloads at his employees and then moves on to bigger things. The "No Answers" approach works only if you are willing to brainstorm with them when they are stumped, and to give them guidance and feedback along the way.

- ***See them as colleagues, not just subordinates.*** Show it by occasionally doing work that may seem "beneath you." Working side-by-side with your employees will strengthen your relationships and increase their respect for you.

- ***Listen to and use their ideas.*** Author John Izzo's research suggests that people want a seat at the table. Employees tend to withhold their ideas and they take less initiative to make improvements when decisions are made without their input.

- ***Stop micromanaging.*** Let go. Stop looking over their shoulders. Ask them what level of inspection, critique, or control they *want* you to use as you manage them. Negotiate ways to get quality work done, while letting them do it their way.

- ***Give the spotlight away.*** This may be the toughest of all. As the hero, you may have received the applause from your employees, and they may have credited you with the team's success. Powering down means sharing the stage and the applause with your team members. Ironically, your stock will go up with your employees as you increasingly give them room to perform (and get credit for) brilliant, creative work.

In a major retail chain, managers yield by letting people practice what the employee handbook preaches: "Use your own best judgment at all times." A manager told the story of her employee returning late from a lunch break, out of breath. When asked why she was out of breath (not why she was late), the employee responded, "A pregnant customer ordered a new bathrobe and it just came in. When I called to tell her about it, I found out she went to the hospital this morning to give birth, so I decided to use my lunch break and run it over to her." The customer wrote an appreciation letter to senior management, and the employee received recognition and applause at the next all-hands meeting.

Do you ever see that kind of customer service in a tightly controlled, micromanaged environment? Probably not. And count on it: empowered employees will have great ideas or perspective on tasks you may not have asked them to perform. They will put their own signatures on excellence. They may even take your breath away.

Bottom Line

Yielding will increase the odds of retaining your best people. As you give people more power to create, make decisions, and truly affect the success of the team, their job satisfaction (and your odds of keeping them) will go up. At the same time, your ability to compete successfully and accomplish your business goals will increase. You have phenomenal power to yield. Try it and see what happens.

TWENTY-SIX

GO FOR IT

*Ponder this: How will you sustain your commitment
to engagement?*

This chapter might be the most important one in the book. Why? Because without a focus on continuous improvement and sustainability, the love 'em message and strategies might be just another good idea (flavor of the month). You don't want that to happen! Here's how to sustain momentum and continue to build a culture that attracts, engages and retains the best people.

Zenith = the peak, the summit, the pinnacle, the top, the apex

Have you ever been to a "zenith meeting"? One organization regularly brings three or four teams of people together to discuss how, as individual leaders and as an organization, they can continually improve and stretch and grow. They ask each other, "How might we do better?" "Could we reach higher?" "Where's the peak?" And they ask these questions about all aspects of the business—including the people side of the equation.

Being an amazing leader demands openness to learning and growth. If you're growing, you're more likely to master the challenge of engaging and retaining the people you can least afford to lose. The moment you think you have the engagement equation all figured out, something changes—in the workforce or in the world. Continuous improvement demands that you constantly scrutinize and modify your engagement strategies, given these changes and challenges.

The Gap Between Knowing and Doing

People say that knowledge is power. But we think, "Not really." Not until knowledge turns into action is it power. Jeffrey Pfeffer and Robert Sutton literally wrote the book on this topic.[58] They say, "Managers who turn knowledge into action avoid the 'smart talk trap.' Managers must use plans, analysis, meetings, and presentations to *inspire deeds*—not as substitutes for action."

Here are some approaches to closing the gap between knowing and doing. Choose the ones that fit best for you.

GO TO

Ask
page 1

Check out the REI—again. Look at the Retention Engagement Index (REI) on page xvii. Answer the questions again and see how your answers compare to the first time you took the quiz. Note the topics that have you wondering or wanting to try something new with your team.

Create your to-do list. You do create to-do lists, don't you? Top the list with stay interviews for all talented employees on your team. Listen carefully to their answers and note specific action steps that you and they agree on. Remember to include timelines for taking action!

Try it. Seems obvious. But sometimes, in the context of busy days and business pressures, we just don't get around to trying the new behavior or action. And often it's frankly easier to stick with habit—with how we've always done it. This week, commit to trying just one thing with one employee.

Get feedback. How did the "trying it" work out? How do you know? The best way to find out is to ask. Go public with your plan; tell people what you're working on and how you're trying to be an even more effective leader. Just telling them might enlist their support.

Choose again. The popular American TV psychologist Dr. Phil is known to ask, "So how's that working for you?" The question commonly elicits a laugh from the audience. Sometimes you try out a new behavior or approach and then realize that it just doesn't work for you. Don't give up. Try it again, in a different way or different time. Or think of another action you'll try instead—next week.

Get help. You don't have to go it alone. Assuming (hoping) you have a love 'em manager, turn there for mentoring and coaching as you try out new strategies. Human resources partners, colleagues, and workplace coaches can be great resources as well.

Sustain Your Investment

Think about your most recent diet. You lost the weight—then what? If you went back to the old habits, to the bonbons and beer, the pounds returned. The same can happen as you try out new engagement strategies. Remind yourself to get feedback, to have follow-up chats, to do what you promised someone you'd do. Ask a friend or use technology (your smart phone?) to help you remember what you plan to do and when you plan to do it.

> *Spiking engagement is one thing; sustaining it is another. In the highest-performing organizations, managers pay attention not only to what increases engagement, but also to what sustains it. In a study of 50 global companies, moving from relatively low levels of engagement to high engagement can add more than four percentage points to operating margin, Towers Watson research shows. Companies that further bolster and sustain engagement by enhancing well-being and performance support add another 13 points to their operating margins.[59]*

The return on your investment? Your efforts to boost engagement will benefit your talented people, you, and your organization.

I need to create and sustain an environment that will support creative and gifted people; to create a space where they can do their best work. That includes allowing for time off, for training, for people to explore their interior life. Time to read and reflect, to network, to get outside of the institution, to think of the customer, the patron, the donor.

Psychic support is important and has been vastly underestimated. Beyond a certain point money matters less than the relationship with your boss and peers. Successful leaders keep pushing themselves to more effectively manage the softer elements, the human side of how work gets done.

—Reynold Levy, president, Lincoln Center,
in an interview with Charlie Rose

Bottom Line

Evaluate yourself often and commit to continuously improving. Hold yourself and the managers who report to you accountable for building a workplace so productive and fulfilling that your talented people will want to stay, create, and make their mark. That's the zenith. We wish you well.

—Bev and Sharon

P.S. Please write to us at **www.keepem.com** and tell us what happened.

CALLING ALL MANAGERS OF MANAGERS

A manager is not a person who can do the work better than his men; he is the person who can get his men to do the work better than he can.

—Fred Smith, chairman and CEO, Federal Express

You can't do this alone. You need to count on the managers who report to you to become love 'em leaders as well.

First, send them a clear message about their responsibility to engage and keep talented people. Clearly define retention goals, accountability, and consequences for reaching (or missing) those goals. Here is an example of one senior manager's message, delivered in a company-wide memorandum:

> *The key now is to continue to execute better than anyone else in the industry. I've seen you operate. I know how well you can execute. And I'm confident that you can not only meet the goals your management has set but exceed them. Of course, there are two keys to superb execution. Great management is one. But the other is great people. And today, great people are hard to find. So when we find talented employees, we simply cannot afford to lose them.*
>
> *Along with your regular sales and service goals, I want you to make talent retention a top priority. Remember: No one plays a more important role in talent retention than you. In the eyes of our employees, you are the company. The culture you create in your department—the personal rewards and respect you provide, the time you take to understand and coach each individual on your staff—these are the keys to retaining and motivating*

*our people. We hold each of you accountable for developing and motivating
your people. That's what will make us thrive.*

—*CEO, global insurance company*

Many leaders asked us for more tips about how to help *their managers* effectively engage and retain talent. Scan this list of suggestions and commit to those that make sense and seem doable. Repeat.

Ask

Are the managers *you* manage conducting "stay interviews"? If so, that's outstanding. If not, they need to start. Your job is to teach those you lead how to ask these crucial questions of their talent, how to prepare for employees' responses (including the tough requests) and then how to make something happen! Hold managers accountable for conducting "stay interviews" with all those they hope will stay on the team and in the enterprise. Ask them to share with you the personalized creative strategies they create with their talent.

Buck

Do you hold your managers accountable for the teams they lead? How? You've probably heard the maxim that busy people do what is *inspected,* not necessarily what is *expected.* You can expect—and should find ways to inspect—honest efforts to keep good people, because those people build your business. And if the managers you manage fail to accept that the buck stops with them, *mentor* them, *coach* them and, if necessary, *move* them out of management.

Careers

After you've held the next career discussion with a manager on your team, ask her how the career chats with *her* people are going. What is she learning about what people want next? How can she help job sculpt and develop the talent on her team? Step up the action: include career management goals in performance objectives for next year.

Dignity

This can be one of the toughest challenges for managers of managers. After all, showing respect, valuing diversity on the team, monitoring sloppy moods—all of this may seem difficult to measure and tricky to manage. Yet, it's part of your job. Your direct reports and those who report to them are watching how you deal with the disrespectful manager who reports to you. They want you to exercise courage, to mentor, to require behavior change, and sometimes even to *move* a disrespectful manager out of the role.

Enrich

Enrichment activities are some of the least expensive, most effective of all engagement and retention strategies. Chat about enrichment possibilities with the managers you manage. Help them prepare for the conversations they'll have with their employees. Devote part of a staff meeting to inviting your managers to share creative enrichment activities they and their employees are planning.

Family

What if you're a family-friendly manager, but a manager you manage is not? You can help him change. Be a strong role model. Walk your talk. Your people watch how you prioritize and choose between work and home events and they might just follow in your footsteps. Coach them to flex, to partner creatively with employees as they struggle with work/life balance. If you set the stage, show it can be done and reward family-friendly managers, you'll create a team that's a magnet for talent.

Goals

Sometimes the managers you manage are worried they can't give promotions to their well-deserving stars. And they worry that when they can't offer those coveted moves up the ladder, their talent will disengage or depart. Help them expand the list of options their own employees have for growth and fulfillment. Remind them too that in order to build talent for the enterprise, they might have to let go of people they'd love to hoard.

Hire

Engagement and retention starts with the hiring process. Help the managers you manage do a better job of choosing talent. Consider a training course for how to select the best candidates, collaborate to create interview guides for the next job opening, and join them in the next interview they conduct. Debrief the experience afterwards and help them fine tune their approaches.

Information

How well are your managers handling information-sharing? Do a transmission check (yes, as with a car) to make sure the key points are getting through to the people they manage. Hold them accountable for accurate, timely information sharing. Their employees' job performance and satisfaction depend on it.

Jerk

People watch to see how you deal with jerks at work, especially if they report to you. Mentor them, performance manage them, and if they continue their jerklike behavior—move them out of management.

Kicks

How are the managers you manage doing in the "fun" department? How fun are *you* to report to? Model the behaviors you want from them. One senior leader we met brought his leaders together to discuss and "test-drive" a list of fun activities for the department. Managers took turns demonstrating the activities for all employees in the unit. Expect leaders to *allow* fun to happen on their teams. Do not let them be fun squelchers!

Link

If the leaders who report to you are "nonlinkers," help them learn to link. Their new connections can certainly help them, but will also provide a crucial network for their talented employees to tap into. It may seem counterintuitive, but it's true that people are more likely to stay and produce when they're surrounded and supported by many.

Mentor

As you mentor them, ask how they're mentoring their employees. Tell them honestly what you see them modeling (the good and the not-so-good) and brainstorm ideas for improvement. Ask them for feedback about your mentoring skills—in what ways do they hope you'll get even better at this vital task?

Numbers

Devote one staff meeting to the cost of loss. Have each of your managers think about the recent loss of one talented individual and, using the list on page 135, calculate the actual cost of losing the employee. Encourage and incent your managers to reduce regrettable turnover, just as you expect (and inspect) every other cost-cutting measure in your organization.

Opportunity

The managers you manage may not be opportunity mining with their talented people. Why? Because they're afraid of losing their best people. An Amazon.com executive said, "We hire ambitious people. If we don't help them grow here—soon—we'll lose them." There you have it. Help your managers find opportunities inside your organization. They might occasionally lose talent from the team, but they'll save it for the enterprise.

Passion

Ask the managers you manage, "Do you know what your people are passionate about?" If they answer yes, ask how they're helping their talent get more of that at work. If they answer no, encourage them to find out—to learn what makes their best people jump out of bed in the morning to bring their best to work. Knowing that will help your managers engage and keep talent.

Question

Are the managers you manage bound by the rules? By *your* rules? If they are, their teams may be less creative and productive than they could be. Check out how you're modeling effective rule-bending. Then expect and support your managers to model—and so encourage—questioning the rules. Which ones no longer make sense? Invite your managers to have a "silly rules" chat at the next staff meeting.

Reward

Notice how the managers you manage are rewarding their talent. Ask them their favorite ways of recognizing all-out effort and work well done. If they clearly have to search for an answer, it's time to give them some ideas about this crucial aspect of excellent leadership. Oh—and how are you modeling this important behavior? What are they learning from you?

Space

Ask the managers you manage to take the space quiz on page 185. Invite them to share their scores. Then, have a discussion. Why did they score as they did? Help them consider multiple ways of giving space in your department, given the culture and the work people do. Request that they, like you, ask "what if?" before saying no when a talented employee makes an unusual request.

Truth

On your organization's most recent satisfaction survey, employees asked (again) for more feedback about their performance, their strengths, and their weaknesses. How do we know that? Because it happens almost every time, in every industry and every country. For many reasons, the managers you manage may not be giving their talented people feedback honestly or often enough. Remind them, model it for them, and hold them accountable for ongoing, supportive, effective truth telling.

Understand

Engage the managers you manage in a listening challenge for a month. Find out which listening tips and tricks work best for you and for them. Have managers make their own specific commitments. After a month, ask them to get feedback from employees. Has anything shifted? Who might win the "best listener" contest?

Values

Does your own organization have a published set of values hanging on a wall somewhere? In your annual report? On your website? Ask your managers if they feel these are the values your organization espouses or actually practices. Ask for some examples of both. Discuss the values they believe are alive and well in your own department. And ask what you can do, in concert with them, to reconcile any values disconnects. Then they'll be ready to do the same with their talented people.

Wellness

Take a stand to increase wellness on your team. Coach the managers who report to you. Reward and hold them accountable for reducing, not increasing, the stress of their workers. Caring about employees' well-being should not be an afterthought. It is central to the role of a manager and belongs in the top line of the position description.

X-ers and Others

Some of the managers you manage think that this chapter is all about pandering. You need to help them see how managing generational differences is a part of strategic management. Initiate a conversation with your managers about the workforce they manage. What differences and similarities do they see across generations and what are the implications for them, as leaders?

Yield

We dare you to ask the managers who report to you if you micromanage them. If they nod their heads, seek specific examples. Ask, "When do I micromanage? What does it look like? Feel like? And what would success look like—you know, if I were perfect?" Now go through the same exercise regarding *their* tendency to micromanage. Having a frank conversation about this topic will put yielding on the radar screen. You and the managers you manage can help each other become even more effective by learning to yield.

Zenith

Invite the managers you manage to join you in the Zenith proposition. Ask them how they can continually improve as managers, thereby increasing employee engagement and retention. Follow up with them and measure their progress. Expect them to sustain their commitment to talent engagement. Your and your organization's competitive advantage depends on it!

And the Final To Do

Dedicate time to having a talent management dialogue with the managers you manage. Here are some questions you might ask.

How will *you*

★ compete for talent differently?

★ better manage the "jerks" who report to you (those managers who don't treat their people well)?

★ help your managers consider engagement and retention strategies beyond pay and perks?

★ reward managers for taking risks to engage and retain talent?

★ hold managers accountable for engagement planning and action?

★ help managers broaden their perspective of who belongs in the "star" category?

★ support the continual engagement/retention training for leaders at all levels?

★ bring our ideas to the attention of those senior to us? How will we influence them to take action?

★ know if we are successful?

★ sustain this initiative?

If you manage people who manage people, you not only have the task of engaging and retaining the talent on *your* team, but also of helping them do the same with their direct reports. Ensure the love 'em message and strategies cascade down to all levels of leaders. Model the actions you want them to adopt. Catch them *in the act* (thanks, Ken Blanchard) of putting those new behaviors into practice.

NOTES

1. Frederick Herzberg, B. Mausner, and B. Snyderman, *The Motivation to Work* (New York: Wiley, 1959).

2. *Turning Around Employee Turnover* by Jennifer Robison, May 2008, http://businessjournal.gallup.com/content/106912/turning-around-your-turnover-problem.aspx.

3. *Aligning Rewards with the Changing Employment Deal* by Watson Wyatt, www.worldatwork.org/waw/adimLink?id=17180 (p. 6).

4. *Employee Engagement A Review of Current Research and Its Implications* by John Gibbons, November 2006, http://montrealoffice.wikispaces.com/file/view/Employee+Engagement+-+Conference+Board.pdf.

5. *Employee Engagement: Has It Been a Bull Market?* by Jennifer J. Deal, Ph.D., Sarah Stawiski, Ph.D., and William A. Gentry, Ph.D., July 2010, p. 3; www.ccl.org/leadership/pdf/research/EmployeeEngagement.pdf.

6. Robert I. Sutton, "Why Good Bosses Tune In to Their People," *McKinsey Quarterly,* August 2010.

7. Adapted from "CareerPower® Classic: A Guide to Development Planning," Career Systems International, Scranton, Pennsylvania, 2011.

8. "They're Not Employees, They're People," *Harvard Business Review,* February 2002.

9. Personal conversation with R. Roosevelt Thomas Jr., author of *Beyond Race and Gender: Unleashing the Power of Your Total Workforce by Managing Diversity* (New York: Amacom, 1991).

10. Marilyn Gardner, "Robin Koval, Advertising Executive at Work, 'Nice' Is on the Rise," *Christian Science Monitor,* October 17, 2006.

11. "2001 Randstad North American Employee Review" (Atlanta: Randstad, 2001); available by calling (877) 922-2468.

12. *Numerical and Functional Labour Flexibility at Firm Level: Are There Any Implications for Performance and Innovation?* by Swiss Federal Institute of Technology No. 80, September 2003.

13. *Work/Family Programs That Work* (Chicago: Lawrence Ragan Communications, 2006).

14. See Priyanka Vyas, "Looking to Give That Edge," *Hindu Business Line,* March 12, 2007, www.blonnet.com/ew/2007/03/12/stories/2007031200050200.htm.

15. Adapted from "The Decision Grid," the Jordan Evans Group, 2013.

16. Marian Ruderman, Laura Graves, and Patricia Ohlatt, "Family Ties: Managers Can Benefit from Family Lives," Center for Creative Leadership, January/ February 2007.

17. Jack Stack and Bo Burlingham, *The Great Game of Business, Expanded and Updated: The Only Sensible Way to Run a Company* (New York: Crown Business, 2013).

18. Chief Learning Officer, Solutions for Enterprise Productivity, "New Survey Reveals Extent, Impact of Information Overload on Workers," October 28, 2010.

19. "Bad Bosses Damage Health, Quality of Life," *The Times of India,* February 5, 2013.

20. Edward P. Lazear, Kathryn L. Shaw, and Christopher Stanton, "The Value of Bosses," August 15, 2012; available at SSRN: http://ssrn.com/abstract=2131572 or http://dx.doi.org/10.2139/ssrn.2131572.

21. For more information, see "Retention Deficit Disorder," Career Systems International, Scranton, Pennsylvania, 2003.

22. Warren Bennis, "News Analysis: It's the Culture," *Fast Company,* August 2003.

23. Robert Sutton, "Building the Civilized Workplace," *McKinsey Quarterly* 2 (December 7, 2007).

24. Robert Sutton, *The No Asshole Rule: Building a Civilized Workplace and Surviving One That Isn't* (New York: Business Plus, 2007).

25. David Dorsey, "Andy Pearson Finds Love," *Fast Company,* August 2001, p. 78.

26. PRNewswire, "Southwest Airlines Reports Increase in Annual Profits; 40th Consecutive Year of Profitability," Dallas, January 24, 2013.

27. *Gallup Business Journal,* "Item 10: I Have a Best Friend at Work," 1999, http:// businessjournal.gallup.com/content/511/item-10-best-friend-work.aspx.

28. "In Today's High-Tech Economy, Employees See Productivity as Increasingly Relationship-Driven and Work as Highly Social, SelectMinds Study Finds," *Business Wire,* October 30, 2006.

29. Calling Brands, *Crunch Time: Why We Need Purpose at Work,* 2012, www .callingbrands.com/sites/all/themes/zen/dave/pdf/brand_china.pdf, p. 13.

30. PricewaterhouseCoopers, *Millennials at Work: Perspectives from a New Generation,* 2008, www.pwc.com/gx/en/managing-tomorrows-people/future-of-work/pdf/ mtp-millennials-at-work.pdf, p. 5.

31. Alison Overholt, "Creating a Gem of a Career," *Fast Company,* March 2006, p. 135.

32. Daniel Goleman, *Emotional Intelligence: Why It Can Matter More Than IQ*, 10th Anniversary Edition (New York: Bantam Books, 2006).

33. Paul G. Stoltz, *Adversity Quotient* (New York: Wiley, 1999).

34. Adapted with permission from "Run the Numbers," Career Systems International, Scranton, Pennsylvania, 2000.

35. Jude T. Rich, "Sitting on a Gold Mine: Reducing Employee Turnover at All Costs," *World at Work,* 2nd quarter 2002.

36. *Gallup Business Journal,* "What Your Disaffected Workers Cost," 2001, http://businessjournal.gallup.com/content/439/what-your-disaffected-workers-cost.aspx. Supported by Towers Watson, *Global Workforce Study,* 2012, http://towerswatson.com/assets/pdf/2012-Towers-Watson-Global-Workforce-Study.pdf; and The Conference Board, *Employee Engagement: A Review of Current Research and Its Implications*, 2006, http://montrealoffice.wikispaces.com/file/view/Employee+Engagement+-+Conference+Board.pdf, p. 17.

37. Edward F. Murphy, *2,715 One-Line Quotations for Speakers, Writers, and Raconteurs* (New York: Crown, 1981), p. 148.

38. Po Bronson, *What Should I Do with My Life?* (New York: Random House, 2002), p. 363.

39. Marilee Adams, *Change Your Questions, Change Your Life* (San Francisco: Berrett-Koehler, 2009).

40. RedBalloon, *2012 RedBalloon Reward and Recognition Report,* 2012, p. 13, www.redballoon.com.au/media/corporate/images/Reward_&_Recognition_Report_2012_RedBalloon_for_Corporate.pdf.

41. *Canadian HR Reporter,* May 8, 2012.

42. Eurofound, *Fifth European Working Conditions Survey*, 2012, Publications Office of the European Union, Luxembourg, www.eurofound.europa.eu/pubdocs/2011/82/en/1/EF1182EN.pdf.

43. Pamela L. Van Dyke, "How to Lead in a Virtual World," *Chief Learning Officer,* January 30, 2013, clomedia.com/articles/view/how-to-lead-in-a-virtual-world.

44. See www.b-society.org/research.

45. Gallup, "Recognition and Feedback Lacking," www.businessjournal.gallup.com/content/146996/employees-need-know.aspx.

46. Michael Griffin, "Open-Door Policy, Closed-Lip Reality," Corporate Executive Board, October 18, 2011.

47. Robert B. Catell and Kenny Moore, with Glenn Rifkin, *The CEO and the Monk: One Company's Journey to Profit and Purpose* (Hoboken, NJ: Wiley, 2004), p. 235.

48. Nic Patton, "Dr Jekyll at Home, Mr Hyde at Work," *Management-Issues,* April 5, 2007.

49. Jim Kouzes and Barry Posner, *The Leadership Challenge*, 4th ed. (San Francisco: Jossey-Bass, 2008).

50. See www.workfittreadmill.com/product.php.

51. Ken Nowack, "Power Napping and Performance," February 8, 2011, http://results.envisialearning.com.

52. See http://business.time.com/2012/04/26/stop-working-more-than-40-hours-a-wek/?utm_medi.

53. See http://www.sbnonline.com/2011/03/take-control-of-your-health-and-well-being/.

54. *What's Next, Gen X? Keeping Up, Moving Ahead, and Getting the Career You Want* (Boston: Harvard Business Press, 2010), p. 60.

55. Susan Mitchell, *American Generations: Who They Are, How They Live, What They Think* (Ithaca, NY: New Strategist, 2005).

56. Adapted with permission from The Learning Café, 2013, www.thelearningcafe.net.

57. Adapted with permission from The Learning Café, 2013, www.thelearningcafe.net.

58. Jeffrey Pfeffer and Robert Sutton, *The Knowing Doing Gap: How Smart companies Turn Knowledge into Action* (Boston: Harvard Business School Press, 2000).

59. Towers Watson, *Global Workforce Study,* p. 8, 2012, http://towerswatson.com/assets/pdf/2012-Towers-Watson-Global-Workforce-Study.pdf.

ACKNOWLEDGMENTS

When we first wrote *Love 'Em,* we never dreamed we'd be invited to deliver five successive editions. Each time we looked at our material, we wondered what more we could say. Each time we found much more to say, and the task became whittling it down.

The job becomes easier, though, when you have a great team of colleagues to support the effort. We could not have managed this task without Nancy Breuer, our awesome "voice editor" who coached us on each edition and (ever so politely and lovingly) told us where we just didn't make sense! She also helped us capture and edit out our U.S.-centricities.

We very much appreciated the work of our colleague Bette Krakau. In addition to being a very experienced consultant and facilitator, she is an avid reader. When we needed someone to find us a fact or bring us up-to-date on an idea, Bette knew just where to search. She also helped us use social media to support our ongoing research into *why people stay* in organizations. Her help and support was invaluable. Lindsay Watkins went the extra mile and supported our efforts from beginning to end.

Steve Piersanti, president of Berrett-Koehler, became our mentor, guide, and speaker-of-the-truth for the fifth time. He read every chapter, applauded when he loved our changes, and gave us very specific feedback when he disagreed with us. His calls always buoyed our spirits.

Artist Tracy Rocca updated the fifth edition artwork, from the cover to icons to Alas story windows. She gave our book a new feel, while staying true to the Love 'Em or Lose 'Em brand.

Once again, the amazing facilitators, coaches, and consultants from Career Systems International delivered our workshops and webinars to organizations around the world. They also trained many internal facilitators who brought their own knowledge to their organizations as they tailored the messages to be culture-specific. As a past client and now the current VP of Product Development and Marketing, Beverly Crowell led our effort to continually improve our wide array of solutions and our consulting approach. She breathes life into everything she does.

With this fifth edition, we set out to truly honor the global reach of this book. We've marveled at seeing each of the 25 translations fill our shelves. To help us add global examples, we decided to call on colleagues, workshop participants, and certified Love 'Em facilitators from around the world. We asked them to provide some examples, stories, and research on their favorite chapters from their own country experience. We received a great deal of excellent information and, alas, could not include it all. We will be putting information on our website to continue to support our global partners.

We appreciate those global clients who delivered our learning solutions to their organizations worldwide and gave us feedback. Special thanks to facilitators from Ingersoll Rand, First Data, and PepsiCo. We also thank the many global Love 'Em users who contributed specific facts and stories. Thank you, Michael Zollinger of Switzerland; Neal Black from Canada; Grace Cheng from Taiwan; Dennis Metcalf and Dang Metcalf of Japan, Korea, and China; Vinnie Chi of Hong Kong; Joyce Jow and Lemuel De Velez of Asia; Matt Hawkins of New Zealand; Elaine Walker of Russia; Caroline Lazarte of Peru; Paul Cheesman in the United Kingdom; and Marie Dell from South Africa. A particular thanks goes out to Alyson Margulies, Michelle Prince, Shelby Moran, and Mary Scarborough for their global perspectives.

A very special note of thanks also goes to Lee Kang Yam, Lucy Lei, and Wendy Tan of The Flame Center in Singapore for their extraordinary contributions based on their perspectives from delivering these messages in Asia.

Finally, we again came to appreciate each other. We have very different skills, very different styles, very strong beliefs, and very packed schedules. We managed to invent a new tempo that truly worked for both of us and, we believe, made this the best edition yet. For all the evening and weekend telephone calls, and the whirlwind of chapters that flew back and forth, we thank our cell phones, our iPads, our patient spouses (Mike and Barry), and each other.

INDEX

ABOUT THE AUTHORS

The authors of this book began their journey together in 1997, when they conducted research for the first edition of *Love 'Em or Lose 'Em*. They were passionate about providing managers with practical tools and strategies for engaging, developing, and retaining the talent on their teams. They still are.

Beverly Kaye founded Career Systems International (CSI) more than 30 years ago, and it has become a global leader in developing and delivering innovative and action-based talent management solutions. With an emphasis on engagement and retention, as well as its flagship offerings in career development,  Career Systems International supports organizations, including more than 60 percent of Fortune's Top 1000 companies, in their talent strategies.

She was recently honored as a "Legend" by the American Society for Training and Development (ASTD) for her ground-breaking and continual contributions to workplace learning over the past two decades. Her first book, *Up Is Not the Only Way,* continues to be a classic in the career development field.

Before earning a doctorate at UCLA, Bev completed her graduate work in organization development at the MIT Sloan School of Management and earned a master's degree from George Washington University.

Bev is a transplanted Jersey girl who has made her home in Los Angeles with her husband Barry, daughter Lindsey, and dog Roxy. Please visit Bev at her company's website, http://CareerSystemsIntl.com, or e-mail her at HQ@CareerSystemsIntl.com.

Sharon Jordan-Evans, president of the Jordan Evans Group, is a pioneer in the field of employee engagement and retention. She works with the people companies can least afford to lose—their high performers.

Sharon is a sought-after keynote speaker for Fortune 500 companies such as American Express, Boeing, Disney, Microsoft, Lockheed, Monster, and Universal Studios.

She has a master's degree in organization development and is a certified executive coach.

Sharon also serves as a resource for a number of national media, including National Public Radio (NPR), *Business 2.0, Chief Executive, CIO, Harvard Management Update, Working Woman, Investor's Business Daily, Business Week,* and the *Los Angeles Times.*

Sharon was born in the Northwest and now lives in Cambria, California, with her husband Mike and a very smart Shih-Tzu named Oreo. She has four grown children and five adorable grandchildren.

To learn more about Sharon's work and to view her speaker video, visit her website at www.jeg.org. To contact Sharon, please e-mail her at sharon@jeg.org.

The Next Time You Need a High-Level Keynote Speaker . . .

. . . you'll want someone who can excite the crowd and mobilize action. Bev and Sharon have spoken at hundreds of mission-critical events, and their clients give them rave reviews.

Engage Sharon or Bev to educate and motivate your audience with topics like these:

- *Love 'Em or Lose 'Em: Getting Good People to Stay*

- *Engagement, Development, and Retention of Key Talent*

- *Engaging the Massive Middle*

- *Keeping the Keepers: A Crucial Leadership Responsibility*

- *Both Sides Now: Manager and Employee Roles in Workplace Satisfaction*

- *High-Performing Leaders Give Attention to Retention*

If you're interested in Sharon or Bev as keynote speakers for your organization, contact Sharon at sharon@jeg.org or Bev at HQ@careersystemsintl.com.

BEYOND THE BOOK

Organizations that grow their people grow their business. And employee engagement and retention thrive in cultures that are truly talent focused. So how do you make it happen?

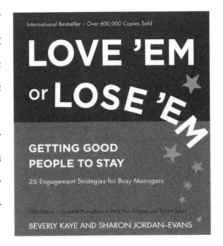

Building and maintaining a talent-focused culture requires a process, not a single event. It also requires a shared responsibility among senior leaders, managers, and employees.

It's not enough to provide key players with a model and some tools. You need the right model. You must align all the key players and cultivate true partnerships with a framework that flexes to your needs. And the tools must be just as practical as they are effective.

We've continued our research about what engages and retains talent (visit www.keepem.com) and applied those findings to the development of a full range of systemic solutions, assessments, tools, and learning experiences offered in the latest modalities for today's modern workforce, including the following:

- **TalentEdge™**, a consulting process that provides a step-by-step flexible strategy tailored to your organization's specific engagement and retention needs. Built on wide experience, it includes recommendations for diagnosing, designing, and delivering as well as sustaining the entire effort and tracking results.

- **Love 'Em or Lose 'Em®: Retention and Engagement for Managers**, a learning solution that refocuses managers' attitudes about talent. It is based on the concepts of *Love 'Em or Lose 'Em: Getting Good People to Stay*. Managers assess their own talent risks and prepare for powerful "stay interviews" as they build their individualized engagement and retention plans.

- **SatisfACTION Power®**, a learning solution that provides employees with the best concepts and strategies of *Love It, Don't Leave It: 26 Ways to Get What You Want at Work*. It helps employees identify ways to make the jobs they have, the jobs they love.

- **The EngagementEdge™ Survey**, an online assessment that offers diagnostic insights to target your specific engagement and retention efforts, while providing a convenient way to measure organizational change.

- **The Love 'Em® at Work Web Portal**, a web-based portal for manager workshop participants to access information, tools and thought-provoking ideas to sustain their learning experience.

- **The Talent Risk Assessment Matrix™**, an interactive tool to help managers assess direct reports on their value to company and risk of departure, and provides a customized list of actionable strategies for lowering or eliminating the risk of departure.

Find more information about these and other engagement and retention solutions by contacting Bev's company, Career Systems International (CSI), at HQ@CareerSystemsIntl.com. Or call (800) 577-6916.

And remember: to learn more about employee engagement and retention, visit Sharon and Bev's joint website, www.keepem.com.

Career Systems International

In 1975, Beverly Kaye founded Career Systems International (CSI) with a vision to become the world's leading provider of career development and engagement and retention products and services. Our foundational premise: improve the workplace for every employee—from senior leaders to the front line—by creating simple training tools and processes that fuel human curiosity. Ignite passion. Unleash potential.

Today, CSI boasts one of the largest, most successful arrays of cross-cultural talent management solutions in the global market. All of our solutions are deliberately flexible by design. We offer multiple certifications, cutting-edge multimodal training, virtual and classroom experiences, and powerful tools both on and offline—all to appeal to the learning preferences of today's diverse, multigenerational workforce.

And while a lot has changed over the past 30 years, some things are constants: our shared belief about the nature of work and relationships, and our belief that people should find meaning and purpose in their work and have the opportunity to make their optimal contribution to the organization's success. This is what guides our every innovation and drives our clients' success.

Read more at http://careersystemsintl.com.

Jordan Evans Group

Fortune 500 companies hire the Jordan Evans Group to work with the people they can least afford to lose—their high performers. That work is available as

- executive coaching for individuals and teams, and
- keynote presentations to motivate, educate, and entertain.

With over 20 years of experience working with executive teams and key leaders at all levels, the Jordan Evans Group helps companies engage, develop, and retain talent, and improve bottom-line results in the process.

Read more at www.jeg.org.

Also by Beverly Kaye and Sharon Jordan-Evans

Love It, Don't Leave It
26 Ways to Get What You Want at Work

Whether for fear of an uncertain economy or reluctance to deal with the inevitable stresses of looking for work, many people feel unwilling or unable to change jobs. So they simply "quit on the job." They disengage, produce less, and bide their time in quiet dissatisfaction, making themselves, and often their coworkers, family, and friends miserable. But there is an alternative.

Love It, Don't Leave It provides readers with 26 ways to make their current work environment more satisfying. Presented, like *Love 'Em or Lose 'Em*, in an appealing, accessible A-to-Z format, *Love It, Don't Leave It* includes strategies for improving communication, stimulating career growth, balancing work with family, and much more. Designed for workers at any age and at any stage, *Love It, Don't Leave It* helps people assume responsibility for the way their work lives work. Readers who try just a few of the strategies in this book may find that the job they want is the job they already have.

"Bev and Sharon do it again! In a simple, straightforward way, they take on an important issue: how to make the most of your work environment. I want every one of our associates to read this book."

—Ken Blanchard, coauthor of *The One Minute Manager* and, most recently, *Great Leaders Grow* and *Fit at Last*

Paperback, 216 pages, ISBN 978-1-57675-250-0
PDF ebook, ISBN 978-1-57675-875-5

Berrett–Koehler Publishers, Inc.
www.bkconnection.com

800.929.2929

Berrett–Koehler Publishers

Berrett-Koehler is an independent publisher dedicated to an ambitious mission: *Connecting people and ideas to create a world that works for all.*

We believe that the solutions to the world's problems will come from all of us, working at all levels: in our organizations, in our society, and in our own lives. Our BK Business books help people make their organizations more humane, democratic, diverse, and effective (we don't think there's any contradiction there). Our BK Currents books offer pathways to creating a more just, equitable, and sustainable society. Our BK Life books help people create positive change in their lives and align their personal practices with their aspirations for a better world.

All of our books are designed to bring people seeking positive change together around the ideas that empower them to see and shape the world in a new way.

And we strive to practice what we preach. At the core of our approach is Stewardship, a deep sense of responsibility to administer the company for the benefit of all of our stakeholder groups including authors, customers, employees, investors, service providers, and the communities and environment around us. Everything we do is built around this and our other key values of quality, partnership, inclusion, and sustainability.

This is why we are both a B-Corporation and a California Benefit Corporation—a certification and a for-profit legal status that require us to adhere to the highest standards for corporate, social, and environmental performance.

We are grateful to our readers, authors, and other friends of the company who consider themselves to be part of the BK Community. We hope that you, too, will join us in our mission.

A BK Business Book

We hope you enjoy this BK Business book. BK Business books pioneer new leadership and management practices and socially responsible approaches to business. They are designed to provide you with groundbreaking and practical tools to transform your work and organizations while upholding the triple bottom line of people, planet, and profits. High-five!

To find out more, visit **www.bkconnection.com**.

Berrett–Koehler
Publishers

A community dedicated to creating
a world that works for all

Dear Reader,

Thank you for picking up this book and joining our worldwide community of Berrett-Koehler readers. We share ideas that bring positive change into people's lives, organizations, and society.

To welcome you, we'd like to offer you a free e-book. You can pick from among twelve of our bestselling books by entering the promotional code **BKP92E** here: http://www.bkconnection.com/welcome.

When you claim your free e-book, we'll also send you a copy of our e-newsletter, the *BK Communiqué*. Although you're free to unsubscribe, there are many benefits to sticking around. In every issue of our newsletter you'll find

- A free e-book
- Tips from famous authors
- Discounts on spotlight titles
- Hilarious insider publishing news
- A chance to win a prize for answering a riddle

Best of all, our readers tell us, "Your newsletter is the only one I actually read." So claim your gift today, and please stay in touch!

Sincerely,

Charlotte Ashlock
Steward of the BK Website

Questions? Comments? Contact me at bkcommunity@bkpub.com.

Certified
B Corporation
bcorporation.net